PRICELESS

A LIFE THAT COUNTS FOR GOOD

What Schools Can Do

D_ tom W?.
tt.#
16.17.21

DRAYTON NABERS, JR.
THE HOPE INSTITUTE

SECOND EDITION

PRICELESS: A LIFE THAT COUNTS FOR GOOD

Second Edition

ISBN: 978-0-9836814-6-5

Copyright © 2021 by

Drayton Nabers, Jr.

3300 Dell Road

Birmingham, AL 35223

Published by

Alliance Publishing, LLC

P.O. Box 190405

Birmingham, AL 35219

Book Design: Vic Wheeler

Printed in the United States of America

CONTENTS

PREFACE

The Hope Institute

The Hope Institute is located on the campus of Samford University and works with Samford. The Hope Institute's Executive Director is Dr. Jodi Newton who was formerly a teacher and then principal and then Assistant Superintendent in the Fairfield City Schools. Thereafter, Dr. Newton became Superintendent of the Homewood City Schools where she served for ten years. She is now Professor, Educational Leadership, in Samford's Orlean Beeson School of Education.

Liz Huntley is The Hope Institute's President. I serve as Chairman of the Board.

The Hope Institute created the Hope Leadership Academy, now in its fourth year of classes. In a three-year curriculum, the Academy helps schools become better places for students to learn and for teachers and staff to work. Important as they are, these are secondary benefits of the Academy. The main purpose of the Academy is to teach school leadership how to help develop strong and good character in students, which is the mission of The Hope Institute.

The Hope Institute does not dictate any character initiative for a school. Rather the Academy teaches principles and provides tools and on-site collaboration for schools to use to fashion their own programs at their own pace and within their existing budgets and management structures.

An Opening Thought Exercise

To get our minds on the right track, let's consider a hypothetical situation.

The Smiths, a couple with one two-year-old child, Bobby, have just learned that both of them are infected with a deadly virus and each has less than a month to live. The Smiths have no savings.

There are two relatives who are available to assume responsibility of Bobby.

One, Uncle Donello, is a good man with a strong character. He is a hard-working day-laborer in golf course maintenance. Donello leads a clean life and is a faithful husband to his wife, Beth, of three years. They have no children. He has little education, no debt, no credit cards. Beth works as a house cleaner. Donello and Beth rent a clean, two-room apartment. With both working, they save about twelve dollars a week. If the Smiths leave Bobby with Donello and Beth, Donello knows he will need to work weekends at a grocery store or WalMart. Both Donello and Beth are devout Catholics and active participants in parish activities. They love Bobby and will seek to adopt him. Bobby will be eligible for Medicaid health insurance.

The other potential guardian is Uncle Marcus, age 40, very bright, a Harvard Business School graduate who struck it rich in business life. He has no intention of adopting Bobby but is willing to be a legal guardian. He is divorced, drives a new Porsche, is a fancy dresser and lives in a lavish six-room, downtown condo. Presently he has no job but plenty of assets to manage, enough to support him abundantly for the rest of his life. Though he has shown little interest in Bobby, if the Smiths choose him to be Bobby's guardian, he has offered to create a trust for Bobby to fund all the cost of raising Bobby: nannies, the best boarding schools, tutoring, summer camps, travel, health care, and essentially all that Bobby may want, etc. until Bobby finishes school, including professional school if Bobby desires.

Should the Smiths choose Uncle Donello or Uncle Marcus?

Many would say they should choose Uncle Donello, because love and good character are of an order far above riches, the best private schools and an affluent life. In fact, in a word, their reason to choose Uncle Donello is likely that good character is "priceless."

***

The purpose of this short book is to introduce in nutshell fashion what character is; why schools should seek to help students develop it; how schools should pursue a successful character initiative; and the many benefits to the schools and students from character initiatives.

Throughout the text speaks of schools "helping" students in character development. Character grows in the students' inner beings or souls. No school can make it grow. Schools can only provide the cultures which influence its growth.

This book concentrates more on the "why" of character development – its benefits to students, the adults in schools (principals, teachers, cafeteria workers, bus drivers, etc.) and the school as an institution. These benefits are great and do not get in the way of the academic program. They actually enhance it.

Inside are comments and illustrations from schools whose leaders have attended Hope Academy classes. Other books provide excellent instruction on programs, teaching ideas and techniques to help in character development. Three good ones are Thomas Lickona, *Character Matters*; Marvin Berkowitz, *You Can't Teach Through a Rat* and Karen Bohlin and Kevin Ryan, *Building Character in Schools*. Hope Academy sessions will involve much discussion of these programs and ideas.

School character initiatives do not guarantee success with all students. The perennial issue of heredity vs. environment, nature vs. nurture, is in play. For reasons no one fully understands, some students will take more readily to a life of virtue than others. There will be successes and disappointments. The challenge for schools is never lose sight of, and always strive for, the goal of a character that counts for good for every student.

Ben White is Assistant Principal of Walker Elementary in Tuscaloosa County. He tells HI: The character education program at Walker Elementary has had a tremendous impact on our faculty, staff, parents and community. Our discipline problems are a fraction of what they were four years ago. Not only that, but our students are kinder to each other. Our students are able to identify character traits; not only identify character traits but they also can describe them and they also look for ways to exhibit these traits in our school. We've also become more service oriented. The character education program has had a major impact in our local community. Because of character education our classrooms, our students, our teachers have looked for ways to actively engage with our community partners. This has had a tremendous impact on all that we do at Walker Elementary.

CHAPTER 1

INTRODUCTION

Perhaps we get ahead of the text, but first offer a short answer to the question begged by the title of this book: what does "priceless" mean in relation to "a life that counts for good"? It does not mean that such a life is rare like a "priceless" diamond. If we look around we can easily find people with lives that count for good. What "priceless" in the book's title means is that a life that counts for good is greatly to be desired and no amount of money can buy or create it. Cultures, most especially family, school and faith-based organizations enable the virtues for a life that counts for good – meaning it has value and significance for goodness. Those who have such lives may not be rich, prominent nor the smartest. They are simply "good," genuinely concerned about others in thought and deed. They are humble, responsible, trustworthy, productive, and have integrity. Through schools which commit to help form the character of students, it is The Hope Institute's goal that these "priceless" lives will abound.

* * *

The essential foundation of any school character initiative is the belief that every student is meant to, and should, count for good. Educating the mind is very important. The Hope Institute believes that helping every student grow in character to pursue a life that counts for good is also a critical responsibility of every school.

Understanding that good character is essential for a flourishing life has been at the heart of ethical thought for 2500 years. And for hundreds of years educators in America understood that education had two great goals - to help children become smart and to help them become good. But in the last fifty years, for many reasons, the nation has lost the conviction that helping children become good, helping them form characters that enable them to count for good, is a fundamental school purpose.

No one needs to make the case for academics in schools. That is accepted by State Boards of Education, local boards, principals, teachers, the media and parents. But character? Schools do not exist for character formation, we hear. It is said that attention to good character growth would be an "add-on" to teacher loads already too burdensome; or it is believed that schools do not have the time or the budget; or that character is a moral thing, something best left to the home, other nonprofits, or places of worship.

The Hope Institute thinks not. Virtually all in education and all parents agree that a human child has a soul to be nurtured and needs help to live successfully and happily in all dimensions of life: family, work and community (throughout we use "parents" to include single moms or dads or other primary caretakers). Teachers know that a child is more than a brain on a stick, and that every child in school-age years is morally a work in process. Moral development through character formation ranks in the same or even a higher order than academic progress. The child has a brain to be sure but also a heart, a conscience and free will. Ralph Waldo Emerson, one of America's most esteemed scholars, correctly said, "Character is higher than intellect."[1] Another very smart man, Albert Einstein, agreed: "Most people say that it is intellect that makes a great scientist. They are wrong: it is character."[2] Good and strong character is priceless.

While in school and without, a child's conscience and moral compass are under development with a myriad of choices to live by the truth or a lie, to be lazy or work hard, to be selfish or generous and kind, to bully or be an agent for peace, etc. These choices one by one, bit by bit and over time, will form habits that will last a lifetime and determine the child's destiny here on earth.

And for many students schools are a good, if not the only, place to attend to character formation. The number of school-age children who attend church, or are active in other character-building programs, is greatly diminished over the last fifty years. Also, families no longer function as they once did in a largely agrarian society or in the industrial age. Many children grow up outside a traditional family. Technology, cell phones and iPads, fast foods and automobiles are changing the nation. Two-worker parents have an impact. If schools ever had the luxury of leaving character development solely to parents or others, they do not now.

But the great thing about a school character initiative is that educators have learned that a re-emphasis on the dual task of helping students both academically and in developing good character has revolutionary, positive effects in the school. Academic programs improve; discipline referrals plummet; student morale and motivation is enhanced with increased pride in and affection for the school; teacher confidence, joy and retention is increased; and parental interest and participation is elevated.

The reason, as discussed in Chapter 3, is that a focus on character development begins with laying a foundation based on the school mission and core values around which all activity will be premised. When school culture is built on such a foundation, a virtuous cycle ensues. School leadership adopts a mission and core values in open dialogue with the school community (staff, teachers, other workers, students and parents) and then puts these into practice. The school becomes a better place to teach and learn and for students and teachers to respect one another; there is greater pride in a culture built on a mission and core values admired by all; and there follows a deeper commitment to the mission and core values.

The habits of good character give the strength to overcome obstacles and succeed in relationships and callings. Good character includes the strength to withstand the ordinary impulses students have that entice them to succumb to challenges that have the power to impede if not destroy success and happiness. Parents and caregivers want their children to have good and strong character. And colleges, businesses, hospitals, courts, sports teams, and school faculties all seek fellow workers or colleagues with strong character. Whatever the pursuit, all search for relationships with individuals who have good character. The question is where and how will it be developed and whether schools should be involved.

How is character formed? Students are not born with their characters formed. Left alone, all humans are prone to waywardness. Characters are formed as children develop habits, good or bad. These habits are engendered in large part in the cultures that encompass children as they mature - family, neighborhoods, clubs, gangs, media blogs, places of worship, schools and the like.

Schools that have no programs for character development unavoidably have cultures in which student character is being developed. Every school has a culture, even those who pay no attention to culture. And these cultures, good or bad, strong or weak are forces or wastelands for character development, good or bad, strong or weak. So no educator can truthfully say that a school can escape involvement in the character development of its students. Any school that wants to ignore character is simply allowing its students' characters to develop by unnoticed forces within the school and without, which may well handicap and haunt children as much "Fs" in academic courses or bad grades on standardized tests. But when the school leadership seeks to develop a culture where good character thrives, students will learn more and teachers will find greater satisfaction in their work and pride in their school. Good character, academic success and joy in work are wrapped together.

More Questions

If school leaders accept that character is important and that schools should play a role in its development other questions pop up like, "Can we afford it" and "Can we pile any more on our overworked faculty?" The good news is that an excellent character program can be very affordable and is in fact not burdensome but is synergistic with everything else school leaders and teachers are trying to accomplish.

A character program is not something outside which is added like a new subject to teach. It will become integral to all school activity. A good character program will improve the school in every facet of its activity.

Any financial investment, if need be, can be shared by local businesses and benefactors, school system foundations or covered in whole or in part by federal Title 1 or 2 funds.

So when a school embarks on a character development initiative, the benefits are large and the financial costs are small. In economic terms, there is a great return on investment.

Though schools have an important role to play in student character formation, the family culture is primary in a child's character development. It has the greatest potential to develop strong and good character in students. And in the family, it is the parents who have the most influence on a child's character development. *How to Lead* is a 2020 bestseller that contains interviews of about thirty of the most successful men and women of the last forty years: people like President George W. Bush, Colin Powell, General Petraeus, Oprah Winfrey, Bill Gates, Warren Buffet, Jack Nicklaus and Condoleezza Rice. All of these individuals noted the prominent, positive influence of parents in their development.

For many students, schools build on strong and good character being formed in the family. For others, where family culture is weak or parents are inattentive in influencing good character, the school's role becomes more important and difficult. But the key point is that in strong and good character development, the role of the family should be primary and prominent.

> **Dr. Quintin Lee is Principal of Childersburg High School a Talladega County School.** He tells HI: During the Hope Academy we were able to come together and create plans for our school. Not plans for other schools, not a cookie cutter approach, but we were able to come together and create a plan of action that will best meet the needs that we have for our campus. The Academy gives us the authority and leadership to create a plan for our school. It leads us to an intentional analysis of our school culture. We tear it apart; what's working good, what's not working good, what can we tweak, what can we improve, what do we not need to get rid of, what do the students say about the school, what do the teachers say about the school. The Hope Institute has led us to make an in-depth look at what's going on with the culture of our school so that we make sure we are doing things that will line up with our mission and our values. Just that time alone was refreshing so that we could celebrate the success we have had as a school and also create new goals. The Academy supplied us with systematic approaches to merging character education to our teaching standards and also provided the foundation for my teachers to become leaders. I have eight teachers who have gone through the Academy and each teacher comes back fired up and ready to lead. As a principal that is something that I definitely look forward to because now those teachers can lead and not only are they leading within their classrooms but leading as faculty members.

CHAPTER 2

CHARACTER, VIRTUES, VICES

What is character? It is a word used all the time in business, politics, sports, schools, and talking about family and friends. But few would volunteer to give a definition.

Character can be good or bad, strong or week. Hitler and Stalin had strong characters, but bad ones. George Washington and Mother Teresa had strong characters and good ones.

Professor Marjorie Garber of Harvard recently wrote a book on character and speaks of a "magic quality" of character "so hard to define, but essential to have."[3]

The purpose of this chapter is to help school leadership and teachers understand more fully what character is, how it is developed and how critical it will be for the long-term success and happiness of every student in K-12 schools.

As traditionally understood and in its broadest sense, character relates to how well something fulfills its purpose or function. The purpose of a knife is to cut; a good knife is a sharp knife. The purpose of a piano is to make music. A good piano is capable of beautiful music The purpose of a human being is to live fully and excellently into all that counts for good in all facets of a human life: in family, school or work, community, etc. When school leaders determine that the mission of a school is to help students become

---

smart *and* good, the word "good" relates to the character of the students – preparing students to be really good humans as they mature – not just to know the good but to love it, to desire it, do it and to pursue lives that count for good.

It will be up to school leadership to discuss and determine what it means for a human to pursue a life that counts for good. Perhaps precepts, teachings or stories from moral traditions can be consulted. William Bennett's *Book of Virtues* is an excellent source. Relatives or neighbors can serve as examples. Historical figures, military leaders and sports heroes can be discussed as can characters in the great novels, movies, plays and parables. Why is Abraham Lincoln admired as a good man and President? What character traits did he have? Or George Washington, Dr. Martin Luther King, Mother Teresa or Helen Keller? Why do most consider Adolph Hitler or Judas Iscariot bad men? What character flaws did they have?

The whole process of a school's character initiative will be built on a foundation of those character traits school leaders determine will enable students to lead lives that count for good. From this foundation there is no higher responsibility of the school, its leadership and teachers, than to exert best efforts to help every student develop these character traits and walk in them.

In this regard character is at the center of moral development. Teachers know that it is not enough only to know the good. What is of ultimate importance is to know the good, desire to do the good and, in fact, choose and do the good. Character is about all three: knowledge, desire and action.

The original definition of character in the Oxford English dictionary was "a distinctive mark, engraved or otherwise formed." In this sense, Lincoln's head engraved on a penny is a "character." In the printing world, a "character" is the face of a piece of lead which when covered with ink is "impressed" on a piece of paper to form a letter or other mark.

This understanding of character makes an important point. Character is rather permanent. It is engraved in students' souls. We can compare it to the ingredients in a cake. Character is baked in, and once there, good or bad, it becomes second nature and is not easily removed.

Character is engraved in students by moral habits or settled dispositions, and habits are hard to break. Almost all who have studied character agree that ethical habits begin to form when children are young. As ancient wisdom tells us, "Train a child in the way he should go; even when he is old he will not depart from it." [4]

For a functional definition of character: it is a bundle of habits of the heart, good ones leading to a good life and bad ones leading to flaws that block goodness and happiness.

A short poem, simple as it might be, teaches a lot about character:

Sow a thought, reap an action.

Sow an action, reap a habit.

Sow a habit, reap a character.

Sow a character, reap a destiny.

For students, and everyone else, character formation begins with thoughts given by parents or teachers or learned in community and through experience. From what a student learns follows how the student acts, and acts that are repeated become habits. Moral habits become second nature (baked in) so how a student reacts in small matters or in crucial decisions flows from habits or "settled dispositions." From little things early in life, a student's destiny is being determined. "Sow a character, reap a destiny."

President Reagan, in a commencement address to college students – but just as relevant to students in any K-12 grade – summarized the essence of character – and its importance for all students:

> The character that takes command in moments of crucial choices has already been determined. It has been determined by a thousand other choices made earlier in seemingly unimportant moments. It has been determined by all those "little" choices of years past – by all those times when the voice of conscience was at war with the voice of temptation, whispering a lie that 'it doesn't really matter.' It has been determined by all the day-to-day decisions made when life seemed easy and crises seemed far away, the decisions that, piece by piece, bit by bit, developed habits of discipline or of laziness; habits of self-sacrifice or self-indulgence; habits of duty and honor and integrity – or dishonor and shame." [5]

This is a graphic summary both of how character is formed and of habits, a fundamental source of moral goodness. Aristotle, the Greek philosopher in the 4th Century B.C. and the father of all serious character thought, flatly observed in his *Ethics* that "Moral goodness is the result of habit."[6] Habits, good and bad, will be the foundation of students' moral choices and action.

Character Development is a Long-Term Process

As President Reagan noted, every student's character is being "determined" by thousands of "little choices" made in seemingly unimportant moments over time in the classroom, on the playground, walking to and from school or riding the bus and doing homework. As students mature they develop moral compasses which are continuously being calibrated and recalibrated, and when sometime in the future there comes time for a "crucial choice" all these little choices will have formed dispositions which will drive actions that will be honorable or dishonorable, have integrity or bring shame.

C. S. Lewis, a prolific author and Professor of English literature at Oxford and Cambridge Universities in England, observes:

> "...every time you make a choice you are turning the central part of you, the part of you that chooses, into something a little different from what it was before. And taking your life as a whole, with all your innumerable choices, all your life long you are slowly turning this central thing either into a [worthy] creature or into a [flawed] creature; either into a creature that is in harmony with other creatures, and with itself, or else into one that is in a state of war and hatred with its fellow-creatures, and with itself."[7]

All students every hour of every day are works in process morally, and the culture in schools (which we discuss in Chapter 3) needs to be shaped to help students develop characters to become "worthy creatures" that count for good.

As through practice students develop habits, good and bad, these habits become the strength of character. Habits are powerful. Some habits are chemical, like alcohol or drugs; some are in students' souls, like courage, patience or generosity, but developed by practice they are powerful. And teachers should always be reminded, "The chains of habit are too light to feel until they are too heavy to break."

The formation of character takes years. It begins when humans are young. Habits are under development even in pre-school years. So understood character development and a student's destiny are not mainly a matter of classroom teaching. Choices and actions made in all stages and all spheres of life form the habits that will determine destiny.

Stephen Covey wrote a best-selling book on "restoring the character ethic" entitled *The Seven Habits of Highly Successful People*. On the basis of his research, Covey observed that the "character ethic" with its long-term orientation was accepted for centuries until about the end of World War I when it was replaced by what he calls the "personality ethic" which is based on attitude, style and technique, attributes that can be "put on" quickly. The personality ethic fits well with the mindset of "short-term America," those people who want quick solutions and easy answers. Covey's book is devoted to recovering the traditional understanding of character. So is The Hope Institute.

Covey compares the character ethic to what he calls "the law of the harvest." There is built into nature some things that cannot be shortened. Wheat planted in springtime cannot be harvested in early summer. An orange tree must develop roots, a trunk, limbs and leaves before it is capable of bearing juicy and tasty oranges. Likewise, habits of the heart that contribute to being fully human cannot be formed through an hour lecture, a three-day seminar or a thirty-day plan. School leaders who embark on helping students become "good" must be patient, but the harvest will be worth the wait, even priceless.

Developing strong and good character yields rich rewards, but for most it does not come easy.

Character Develops by Overcoming Difficulties

Scott Peck opened his best-selling book, *The Road Less Traveled*, with these words: "Life is difficult," and continued by observing that "Life is a series of problems...." And it is. Today's students will enter a competitive world and will suffer losses. We all do. Things will rust, wear out and break down. They will have to be fixed. There will be disease; perhaps even a pandemic. Character that counts for good is formed by facing problems head on. The character trait that many assert is a key to success is "grit" (or perseverance or steadfastness or tenacity), the capacity to face and work through obstacles.

Ray Kroc, the founder of McDonald's, had a plaque in his office which carried this message:

> "Nothing in this world can take the place of persistence. Talent will not; nothing is more common than unsuccessful men with great talent. Genius will not; unrewarded genius is almost a proverb. Education will not; the world is full of educated derelicts. Persistence, determination alone are omnipotent." [8]

Those who lead schools in character development should ponder this wisdom.

A great Alabamian, Helen Keller, gives us the same message:

> "Character cannot be developed in ease and quiet. Only through the experience of trial and suffering can the soul be strengthened, vision cleared, ambition inspired and success achieved."[9]

Helen Keller, blind and deaf from a very early age, experienced untold trials and suffering. If a school is serious about helping its students grow in strong and good character, it must continuously challenge its students in its programs, including academic, for life certainly will. Students must learn early to work hard, face challenges directly and persevere to the end. "Give me a stronger back, not a lighter load," good people say. Character is about a stronger back.

Virtues

We turn now to a closer look at habits that strengthen students to become good human beings, to pursue a life that counts for good. These habits are virtues. (We will use "virtue" and its opposite, "vice," in our discussion of character strengths, aware that the words are considered old fashioned by most today. In classrooms, perhaps character strength or trait or quality or "habit of the heart" will work better.)

Virtues are internal capacities engraved in souls by practice to become habits or stable dispositions that enable students to live good lives.

C. S. Lewis tells us what virtue is, using tennis to make the point:

> "There is a difference between doing some particular just or temperate action and being a just or temperate man. Someone who is not a good tennis player may now and then make a good shot. What you mean by a good player is the man whose eye and muscles and nerves have been so trained by making innumerable good shots that they can now be relied on. They have a certain tone or quality which is there even when he is not playing, just as a mathematician's mind has a certain habit and outlook which is there even when he is not doing mathematics. In the same way a man who perseveres in doing just actions gets in the end a certain quality of character. Now it is that quality rather than the particular actions which we mean when we talk of 'virtue.' "[10]

Moving from tennis to golf, Ben Hogan is everywhere recognized as one of the all-time great golfers. Hogan's 240 yard one-iron shot on the 18th hole in the 1950 U.S. Open is one of the most remembered and celebrated shots of all time. The one iron is the most difficult club to hit. Most pros don't even try. The 1950 U.S. Open was the first tournament Hogan had played after a devastating car wreck that had almost killed him. Hogan's one iron shot was on the 36th hole he had played on the final day of the tournament. Hogan was so exhausted he could barely walk. His shot was perfect, not because of lessons Hogan had remembered, but because he had practiced the shot for hours and hours "in seemingly unimportant moments" to quote Reagan. As C. S. Lewis puts it, Hogan's "eye and muscles and nerves had been so trained by making innumerable good shots" in practice and past tournaments as to make the swing automatic.

The muscle memory of the great athlete leads to an understanding of virtue. Virtues apply to the moral life and through practice and repetition provide the built-in wisdom, motivation, readiness and strength to be a good person. Virtues become second nature as the person faces critical decisions, trials and challenges of life.

We need to note two additional attributes of virtues. First, virtues are sources of internal strength. It is easy to overlook that virtues are character *strengths*. There is a tendency today to reduce virtues to values – standards for moral goodness. The words for virtues provide values in the sense they provide guideposts for goodness. The values of justice and kindness, for instance, instruct us to be just and kind. But, as virtues, justice and kindness give us the capacity to be just and kind.

The root of the English word "virtue" is the Latin word, "vir," which connotes strength. The word, "virus," is based on this root as is "virulent" – both connoting power.

Virtues, as habits engraved in our souls, give us the strength to do the things that values instruct us to do.

Second, virtues work to form moral *excellence*. The Greek word for virtue is "arête" which means excellence as well as virtue. Likewise, in English the word "virtue" connotes excellence, and a good character consists of a cluster of virtues that produce excellence in action in every facet of life. The excellent and abundant life consists in virtue.

Character in essence is simply a bundle of virtues and vices. Building good character in students is a matter of strengthening the virtues and poisoning the vices. It's like farming. To have a good crop fertilizer is needed to help the crop become robust and yield nutritious produce while pesticides are needed to kill weeds and harmful insects and molds. And, as we will discuss in Chapter 3, for the harvest to be plentiful, the farmer needs good soil and weather; i.e. a good culture.

We turn now to look at the virtues, and their opposites, the vices.

Tina Towers, Principal, Barkley Bridge Elementary School: Passion Projects became an annual schoolwide event. Students determine what they are passionate about and are grouped with a staff member with related passions. Throughout the year, groups meet to learn, plan, and develop a Passion-to-Compassion service project. Chunking the Chains was one group project in which students raised funds to purchase fence materials so dogs don't have to live attached to a chain. Students wrote letters and presented at the Hartselle City Council meeting to request that a law be put into place that dogs cannot live on chains. Through all Passion Projects, students realized how they can make a difference through the lives of others. They also learned that having a caring heart and showing kind actions can make a difference at Barkley Bridge Elementary and the world around us.

What are the Virtues?

It may be helpful to arrange virtues in four groups along the lines of categories used by the Greeks some 2500 years ago – wisdom (cognitive), justice (relational), courage (performance) and temperance (self-governing).[11] It would be good, but certainly not mandatory, for a school's core values (discussed in Chapter 3) to include at least one virtue from each of these four categories as any strong and good human character will have virtues from all of these groups. Here are lists of virtues that might be helpful though each school may study and discuss more or fewer. They are taken from three books on virtue; Thomas Lickona, *Character Matters*; André Comte-Sponville, *A Small Treatise on the Great Virtues*; William Bennett, *The Book of Virtues*:

LOVE
(The Overarching Virtue)

Cognitive	Relational	Performance	Self-governing
Practical Wisdom	Justice	Courage	Self-control
Contemplative Wisdom	Empathy	Patience	Hope
Humility	Compassion	Resilience	Self-discipline
Good judgment	Caring	Perseverance	Patience
	Respect	Grit	Simplicity
	Honesty	Trust	Moderation
	Integrity	Faithfulness	
	Kindness	Loyalty	
	Generosity	Responsibility	
	Mercy	Positive attitude	
	Gratitude	Hard work	
	Tolerance		
	Gentleness		

The virtues classified here as "relational" are sometimes classified as "moral." That's okay but in a sense all virtues are moral. For instance courage is a moral virtue in that it provides the strength to act morally; to be honest when it hurts or to be kind when it may be unpopular. Likewise, the self-governing virtues are moral; for instance, when they strengthen students to control their temper or be patient.

There can certainly be disagreement as to the categories listed above. For instance, "hope" is listed as a self-governing virtue when some would put it in the performance category. The development of all character rests in the positive attitude or hope that long-term gratification will follow short-term sacrifices, trials and struggles. So often youngsters, who have no hope for tomorrow, will pursue enticing but crippling pleasures today. Hope, or confidence in the future, is essential for all virtue.

Virtues in a Mississippi Community

Clifton Taulbert, born and raised in the Mississippi Delta in the Jim Crow era, has become a national leader in character development in school communities. His wisdom and insights come not from his school experience, which was in impoverished, rural, segregated schools, but from the habits of the heart of adult friends in his "cotton picking" community in rural Mississippi. His leading text for character initiatives in schools is *Eight Habits of the Heart*, which discusses how adults in his community practiced and passed on to him habits of the heart which gave him the character to succeed in life, ultimately being invited to speak to a United Nations assembly and at the United States Supreme Court.

The eight "habits" or virtues Taulbert discusses in his book are: Nurturing Attitude, Responsibility, Dependability, Friendship, Brotherhood, High Expectations, Courage and Hope. It was not formal education – though Taulbert is smart and eloquent – but good habits that empowered Taulbert's success. Born in rural Mississippi in the 1950s, he has counted for good. His book encourages every school leader to understand that good habits, those of the heart, are as vital to success as book learning.

As school leaders talk through which character strengths to empha-size, they should keep in mind that no virtue operates independently of the others. Rather, they work in clusters. There is a tight interdependence among the virtues. We will devote an entire chapter on why love should be the overarching virtue, but while love may be the supreme virtue, it needs the support of others. It needs wisdom – we all know parents who deeply loved children but spoiled them. Wisdom, Hebrew wisdom tells us, "is more precious than jewels and nothing you desire can compare with her."[12] Love needs courage. Courage is essential to all virtues, including love. C. S. Lewis writes, "Courage is not simply one of the virtues, but the form of every virtue at the testing point. ... Pilate was merciful till it became risky."[13] And self-control – without self-control the bonds of love can be snapped in an instant when the vices of lust, greed or anger are at play. Steadfastness or perseverance ("grit") is key to the development of every virtue that might be tested in adversity. And hope is necessary to motivate deferral of keen pleasures today, like drugs or sex, for a better life tomorrow. We could go on...

Vices

There is a shadow side of habits of the soul which is found in vices. Vices are the opposite of virtues except they are strong; in fact, all too often stron-ger than virtues. Vices are internal strengths engraved in souls by practice to become habits or stable dispositions which prevent students from living morally good lives.

And what are the vices? We can divide them into three categories, cold-blooded, warm-blooded and roadblocks. Teachers will find them in students, and unless they are angels, in themselves. In preparing students for an abundant life, the vices (or corrupt character traits) must be poisoned and eliminated:

Cold-blooded	Warm-blooded	Roadblocks
Pride	Lust	Laziness
Conceit	Anger	Dishonesty
Greed	Gluttony	Irresponsibility
Envy		Cynicism
Egotism		Untrustworthiness
Egoism		Distrustfulness
Selfishness		Contempt
Stinginess		Addiction
		Despair

In any frank appraisal of the good life, we will find vice even in the midst of the expression of virtue. A student's ego may well be involved in generosity when it is for show. And kindness may be motivated in part by the expectation of a reciprocating reward. The ultimate good is for virtues to become truly second nature (like breathing in and out) which allows a student to ignore the influence of "self" and become altogether altruistic.

We have observed that as a functional matter, character is a quiver of habits, good or bad, that will determine who students are, how they will respond to the challenges of life, whether they will make a difference for good and ultimately how successful and happy they will be.

The "life that counts for good" is morally good. All virtues contribute to moral goodness. The "life that counts for good" is also productive, contributing wholeheartedly to excellence in whatever pursuit a student engages, in school and beyond. Down through the ages "laziness" has been considered one of the chief vices. All vices hinder individual and group or team productivity; and moral goodness. The good life is balanced: morally good and abundantly active and productive.

Can we refer again to Ralph Waldo Emerson's insight? "Character is higher than intellect." Was he correct?

Our next chapter will turn to school culture. A school's culture will help form the character of students in the way that soil and climate determine the size of a harvest and the taste of the crop.

CHAPTER 3

CULTURE AND CHARACTER

I f a school is to be successful in contributing to the development of good character in students, it must build and then continuously refresh an ethically strong culture. Culture is to the quality of schools in much the same way as character is to the moral strength of students. Cultures, in the school and without, will determine how student character is formed. Professor James Hunter at the University of Virginia, a student of character development, writes that "moral instruction is an exercise in the transmission of culture" and "character is inseparable from the culture within which it is found and formed." [14] A student's character will reflect the cultures in which the student abides.

Culture

The word, "culture," comes from the Latin word, *cultura,* which had both an agricultural meaning – to "tend, guard or cultivate" a garden or field, and a moral connotation as well. Culture can be likened to soil in a field that must be "cultivated" to produce an abundant crop. The farmer works hard as he prepares the field; he plows, removes weeds, fertilizes and then plants. Afterward he awaits the crop, continuing to tend the field.

Beyond this agricultural meaning, *cultura* had a somewhat devotional meaning, "to honor," from which the concept of "cult" derives. Strong cultures like those of the Marines, the New York Yankees and Chick-fil-A are "cult like." They have a "way" about them that shapes the character of troops, players or employees. They are inviolate; in a sense, sacred. Good schools form such cultures, and they become authoritative.

All schools, in fact all organizations, have cultures. They can be positive or negative, strong or weak. A book, *Built to Last*, is about great American companies. In searching for the key to their exceptional performances, the authors devote a chapter to "Cult-like Cultures." The authors reflect in their introduction to a second edition that "We've come to understand… that ultimately this is not a business book, but a book about building enduring, great human institutions of *any* type." (emphasis in text). Great schools, kindergarten to university, need "cult-like cultures." A strong, positive school culture is essential to cultivate and nourish both academic achievement and moral goodness in students

School leaders need to be aware that there are many cultures that can influence students: certainly the family which is where the foundation for character development is laid. All families have cultures, good, bad, weak, strong. And students also have or live in peer groups (perhaps gangs), neighborhoods, villages, churches, cities, states, nations, and national origins which have cultures that influence their characters. Often these other cultures conflict with the school culture which causes difficulties.

Mission Statement

An essential step in creating a strong school culture is adopting a mission statement which declares the purpose of the school. If character development is to be a part of the school's mission, it must be a part of the mission statement.

Dr. Martin Luther King observed: "character plus intelligence – that is the goal of true education."[15] Dr. Thomas Lickona, a mentor of The Hope Institute and for a generation one of the nation's leading advocates of character education, wrote in *Character Matters*, a definitive and highly recommended book on character development in schools, "Down through history all over the world, education has had two great goals: to help students become smart and to help them to become good."[16] This dual purpose of public education was widely recognized and alive going back to our nation's origin and lasting until about the middle of the 20th Century when the purpose of education was seen as more restricted to academics measured by test scores and graduation rates. From about 1990 forward, many educators led by Dr. Lickona have been about the task of reviving character development in pre-K and K-12 schools. Alabama's legislature adopted a policy in 1995 for schools to pay more attention (ten minutes a day!) to a list of virtues. In Washington, D.C., Character.Org has led the way on a national level. The Hope Institute is committed to the renaissance of character development in schools in Alabama.

Another concept that needs to be included in any school mission statement is "excellence." Whatever the challenges, as for the development of character, the goal must always be "excellence" and The Hope Institute is confident that in any school excellence in character development can be achieved. Virtues, which are the muscles of strong character, have always included the notion of excellence. Schools cannot help in the development of strong and good character unless, top to bottom, in all things they are committed to excellence and continuous improvement in all aspects of their activity. Virtue does not thrive in mediocrity.

A California high school principal reflected on his school's mission, noting how easy it is for a focus on character to slip.

"Over time the *de facto* mission of our school had evolved into helping our students get into Stanford. I'd like for us to be asking,

'Are we helping students develop the sense that they are *moral* agents – able to create a better character for themselves and a better world for us all?' "[17]

Such is the key question for every school community. Together with personal academic achievement, students need to develop characters to better serve others, pursuing purposes beyond selfishness when they finish a school (whether it be elementary, middle, high school or college).

Core Values

Along with a Mission Statement, in building a strong school culture every school needs to adopt written core values to guide all activity. (We will refer to the Mission Statement and Core Values together as "Basic Beliefs.") Some find it helpful to discuss and adopt core values before the Mission Statement. Maybe a school might work on both simultaneously. The order is not important. The two must work together. The core values will express the heart of the school's culture which will in turn influence the calibration of the moral compasses of students.

Core Values need to be rather permanent and authoritative. They are not to be easily amended or modified. They stand for: "This is our way." "This is the way we do things." Every thriving and productive community needs foundational values around which all activity is organized. They are like the roots of a tree that will produce much fruit. The drafting and adoption of core values should not be hurried, and should be done with patience and grace.

Andrea Hamner, Principal, Huntington Elementary School: At Huntington, we had honest conversations about where we were in making character education part of every facet of our school day. We found that it is not about a lesson or an activity; it is about a way of life. Our way of life at Huntington is "The Wildcat Way." Our staff realized that modeling must begin with us and we must learn to be honest and kind with each other and with our students and families. Our students have truly bought into "The Wildcat Way," and they have transformed our school into a place that focuses on kindness, compassion, honesty, responsibility, and respect.

The statement of core values can take many forms but focusing on key virtues can be very helpful. (Virtues and values can be called by the same word.) Perhaps core values can include several virtues plus tag lines. For example:

Honesty: we always tell the whole truth.

Perseverance: we finish what we start, on time

Respect for everyone: "It's good that you exist."

Excellence: our very best in everything, always

Self-control: count to ten before reacting

> Cas McWaters, Chief Academic Officer, Cornerstone Schools of Alabama: Character education is life changing when it leads to a "culture of character." When students understand the core values and then internalize them, real character growth occurs. At Cornerstone Schools of Alabama, this internalization has resulted in students seriously evaluating their thinking and actions over time based on the core values. At Cornerstone the deep reflective self-analysis and identification of weaknesses and strengths by a vast majority of the students has been amazing. Students have given testimonies time and time again about the positive changes in their lives revolving around the values of love, responsibility, endurance, integrity, and respect. The change is evident not only in their self-evaluation but also in their behavior and views on life.

Adopting Basic Beliefs

It is very important that there is buy-in to the school's Basic Beliefs from the whole school community – students, leadership, staff, teachers, custodians, bus drivers, cafeteria workers and parents. As students move in and out of the school the student and parent communities will change and school leadership should make every effort to see that the Basic Beliefs are communicated to the new students and parents and to seek to win their understanding and endorsement.

This will take time and effort. A school might use surveys, focus groups, Zoom meetings, videos, one-on-one and in-person group meetings, Twitter, Instagram, etc. There may not be total agreement throughout the community on every word but there will be more agreement than might be expected. Most parents, and most humans, like the concept of Basic Beliefs that express moral truth and are taken seriously. Almost all adults think virtues such as honesty, respect, kindness, responsibility and others listed in Chapter 2 are good, and the vices listed there are bad.

The Basic Beliefs need to be lofty, aspirational and challenging. Human beings, when challenged and led by example, can do far more than might be expected, and nothing is more invigorating to a human being than morally to achieve more than is imagined.

School leadership needs to keep in mind that there are both adult and student audiences to be unified behind Basic Beliefs. Often it is helpful to develop a simple "touchstone" which captures the imagination of students.

The purpose of a touchstone is to express the aspirations of the student community in a few words. The touchstone, "We take the high road," is an excellent one; or for a school whose mascot is the eagle, "We soar like eagles;" or to emphasize excellence and unity, "Excellence Together." School leaders don't need to worry about being original. The purpose is to unite and motivate students. If another school has a great touchstone, work with it.

> **Kelsey Frey, Kindergarten Teacher, Mountain Brook Elementary School:** "Lancers Lead from the Heart" is a touchstone that every teacher, student, and staff member embodies daily at Mountain Brook Elementary. We keep our core values at the center of everything we do and continuously reflect on our purpose to point us in the direction that promotes growth individually and collectively. Positive experiences with character education not only transform the person, it also transforms the school's culture.

The process of determining a school's mission and core values is of paramount importance. Three issues will be involved around which consensus needs to be reached. First, the primary issue of the mission is *what* is the school's purpose; why does the school exist? Second, the primary issue of core values is *how* are adults and students to work together in pursuing the mission? Third, there is the primary issue in leadership: how can students and, indeed, the whole school community, be motivated to put the core values into practice?

It is easy to see how these are the most foundational questions for any school (really any organization). Getting the whole school community, the schools' adults, students and parents in agreement will be the key to the school's success. For if substantial agreement can be reached, the school community can work in harmony to pursue a worthy mission in accordance with core values. The Basic Beliefs become the school's "Way;" ("this is the way we do things"), and as progress is made there is deep satisfaction in the work of the school.

The job of school leadership is to appeal continuously to the aspirations contained in the Basic Beliefs. This should be done in word or deed most every time students, faculty, parents or the neighborhood come together – in assemblies, in the classroom, in sport practices, at graduation, etc. The Basic Beliefs need to become second nature to the whole school community. Over time the schools will have stories of adults and students rising to exceptional heights. Such stories are excellent tools in sustaining the power of the school's culture.

> Dr. John Lowry, Principal, Shades Cahaba Elementary School: Our mission statement, "Shades Cahaba educates, protects, respects, and loves children," provides teachers with a framework from which to treat all students. We create a caring school with invested teachers, exceptional volunteers, and community support. This commitment from our staff, to invest in every student who walks through our door, along with the diverse population we serve, has created a rich environment where opportunities to show good character are abundant and necessary to be successful.

The Spirit and Drive of a School

For many years in the last century, IBM, the most admired company in the world, and its CEO, Thomas Watson, Jr., were at the forefront in emphasizing the power of a company's beliefs. In a famous speech at the Columbia Business School, later published in a short book, *A Business and Its Beliefs*, Mr. Watson declared:

"This, then, is my thesis: I firmly believe that any organization [including schools], in order to survive and achieve success, must have a sound set of beliefs on which it premises all its policies and actions.

"Next, I believe that the most important single factor in [a school's] success is faithful adherence to those beliefs.

"And finally, I believe that if an organization is to meet the challenges of a changing world, it must be prepared to change everything about itself except those beliefs as it moves through corporate life.

"In other words, the basic philosophy, spirit, and drive of a [school] have far more to do with its relative achievements than do technological or economic resources, organizational structure, innovation, and timing. All these things weigh heavily in success.

But they are, I think, transcended by how strongly the people in the [school] believe in its basic precepts and how faithfully they carry them out."[18]

Watson was talking about "any organization." His thesis and its wisdom applies to schools as well as corporations. First, he advised, "have a sound set of beliefs" (adopted after all in the community have been consulted). Second, faithfully adhere to them. Third, stick with them as changes occur about the school, internally and externally, in the neighborhood and in demographics. The Basic Beliefs "transcend;" they bring out the best in students and teachers. They have power in creating a culture that elevates academic success and the character of everyone in the organization.

Building, maintaining and strengthening school culture is the most import-ant task of school leadership. It costs very little but it will require effort, courage, persistence and passion. Its rewards in terms of measurable success and deep satisfaction will be great.

Some will think, "This will get old." It never does. Everyone wants to be a part of a community that "takes the high road," that has core values that bring out the ethical best in students and adults. When the principal, and all in leadership, including teachers, never tire of talking about and practic-ing, (all the time, one on one, in groups and at assemblies, at ballgames and in the cafeterias) excellence, respect, love, responsibility, such core values or others, a school comes alive with achievement in the classroom and on the field of life.

Lisa Holland, Teacher, Shades Cahaba Elementary School: Having all stakeholders invested in using the same language to guide, advise and encourage reflection for students has proven to be a solid backbone to our character education program. The Shades Cahaba Way, (six life values) is used by faculty staff and students to give pause and reflect on healthier choices and thinking in their daily lives at school and at home. As a special area teacher I use these phrases daily with all grade levels resulting in authentic discussions and true understanding of my classroom expectations.

Where to Start

School leadership needs to understand where to start – what are the prerequisites for developing the culture to engender strong character? A good place to begin is the wisdom in the observation of Hal Urban quoted by Dr. Thomas Lickona in *Character Matters*. Both Urban and Lickona have been leaders in character-in-schools discussions for decades. Here is Urban's comment:

"I've had the good fortune to visit schools all over the country that have character education programs in place. The first word that pops into my mind when I visit them is "clean." I see clean campuses and buildings, hear clean language, and see kids dressed cleanly and neatly. I also see courtesy being practiced by everyone – students, teachers, administrators, custodians, and cafeteria workers. Most important, I see teaching and learning going on in an atmosphere that is caring, positive, and productive."[19]

Cleanliness and courtesy are prerequisites to the culture that will generate student character development. Neither cleanliness nor courtesy is a virtue, but both are habit forming, and courtesy readily grows into the virtue of respect, even love. Neither costs much, but both require vigilance and the cooperation of all – principal, staff, teachers and students. No one passes by scraps on the hall floor or paper towels on bathroom floors. Every locker is closed tight. Toilets are flushed. Playgrounds and school grounds need to be free of debris. Foul language is out. Sloppy dressing is taboo. Classrooms and hallways need to be clean and orderly – the work of teachers and students alike.

There will be students or parents who resist. "What difference does it make?" they will ask. Perhaps there may not be any cogent argument that a scrap of paper in the hallway or a vulgar tongue affects learning but they do prevent the growth of character. Leaders need to be patient but persistent. Such is the way of any good institution, school or business students may later be a part of. They need to be prepared. Cleanliness is an essential beginning of any character initiative.

As for courtesy, teachers need to greet students by name with eye contact and a sense of delight, and students need to show respect to all adults, including visitors, and be respectful of all fellow students, especially in class. Again, no cost. In many schools with character initiatives, each student is greeted by name when he or she arrives at school, and at the door of each classroom when entering before a class begins.

Maya Angelou, the great American poet, tried to make eye contact and say "Good morning" every day, to everyone she passed, stranger or friend, rich or poor. That is a great idea, especially in the school. It will brighten and refresh the culture and extend a bond of friendliness throughout.

Dr. John Lowry, Principal, Shades Cahaba Elementary School: Greeted at the entrance and their classroom door, students are surrounded by invested adults. In past years, surveys have shown 99% of parents reported that their child feels safe at school and 97% of parents reported their child feels valued at school.

Of course, cleanliness and courtesy may take time to establish, and schools may have different standards, but without both at the foundation of a school's culture, it will be difficult, really impossible, to move forward.

Urban's statement concludes that he has observed that teaching in schools of character is "caring, positive, productive." These are at the center of a mature school culture.

Perhaps, Hal Urban put the essentials of a successful character initiative in a nutshell. A school needs to be clean, polite, caring, positive and productive. If a school can get these right, it will be a great school, before anyone says a word about teacher credentials, test scores or the building's architecture. The academic dimension of the school will continuously improve, just as tasty fruit is abundant on the vine that is properly cultivated.

Dr. Alicia Hunsberger, Principal, Cahaba Heights Elementary School. Our intentional pursuit of building strong character in our kids has materialized into an ongoing journey where we regularly evaluate our needs, celebrate our strengths, and address identified areas of weakness. Teachers explicitly teach and model strong character through a daily practice of morning meetings we call Heights Huddle. We have created language that supports our core values and enables all stakeholders to have a voice in our students' understanding of individual and collective growth. We have teams who address actionable items to ensure progress in sustaining a culture that elevates character and student engagement. We celebrate student learning, service, and leadership regularly. Our learning is not limited to the walls of the classroom, the standards, the curriculum, or the master schedule. We seek to serve the whole child by providing meaningful learning experiences that are evaluated regularly over time in order that we might, collectively, raise both smart and kind kids at Cahaba Heights.

CHAPTER 4

LEADERSHIP, CHARACTER AND FREEDOM

What is the leadership that helps craft a school's Basic Beliefs and brings them to life throughout the school? We begin discussion by looking at the differences between transactional and transformational leadership.

Transactional/Transformational Leadership

Almost all organizations operate in two dimensions. One can be called transactional. Businesses offer a product or service and attract a customer to buy it at a price that generates a profit. This "transaction" is in the transactional dimension. This dimension is critically important. Businesses must succeed, even grow, at this level or they do not survive. A nonprofit organization provides a product or service but cannot generate profits from those served and therefore, at the transactional level, must find donors to fill the gap. The measure of businesses at the transactional level is usually monetary. For a sports team, it is in wins and losses. Continuous improvement at the transactional level is essential in any organization, and school leaders must insist on it.

The second dimension is called transformational. This is the dimension that was the subject of Mr. Watson's lectures at The Columbia Business School. It is in the organization's beliefs, its "basic philosophy, spirit and drive." It transcends the transactional; it's about the ethical values and transcendent moral purposes of an organization – about a school's Basic Beliefs.

Grantland Rice, the great Alabama sports writer, was a poet as well. He wrote about the transformational dimension:

"When the Great Scorer comes to mark against your name; It matters not that you won or lost but how you played the game."

In character development, it's not wins and losses but transformed lives that are ultimately important.

For public schools, in the transactional dimension the government collects taxes and passes on revenues to schools that are expected to educate students. The government draws geographical lines for enrollment, requires students to enroll, specifies what to teach, how to administer discipline, how many days and hours of classes schools must provide teaching, and measures academic success primarily with test scores and graduation rates. Personal relationships can be secondary. In the classroom, lessons are taught, tests are taken and grades are given. There are many challenges, perhaps today more than ever. Bureaucracies are built; there is monotony, pressure, teacher dissatisfaction and burnout. Such is the transactional dimension in schools.

There is a transformational dimension to teaching that provides deep personal rewards, satisfaction and joy, but today it is at risk of being suffocated by the pressures in the transactional sphere. The transformational dimension is in the second prong of the dual purpose of education, "intelligence *plus* character" as Dr. King put it. Character development is where principals, teachers, staff, bus drivers, custodians, kitchen workers and all others become transformational agents. It is where deep joy in education can be found.

Transformational leaders are servant leaders. They understand that their work is a calling to serve young humans with a soul and guide and enable them to aspire to and live a life that counts for good. Basic Beliefs are the transformational dimension's oxygen. Basic Beliefs help form the culture in which students can develop good character. Basic Beliefs unite the school, teachers and students in a worthy mission with core values, and the great thing about Basic Beliefs is that a stronger transformational culture produces not only growth in good character in the students but at the transactional level better test scores and human beings better prepared to meet and overcome the challenges of the world beyond self and school – and teacher joy and satisfaction.

In businesses, profit and nonprofit, and in sports teams as well there can be great emphasis on the transactional (profits, wins and losses) and much early success, but too often there follows exhaustion and burnout when the "bottom line" eclipses the transformational part. The great executives, coaches, principals, teachers and school workers cherish the culture that transforms as well transacts.

> **Wendy Crow, Teacher, Hartselle Intermediate School:** I was at that critical stage of teacher burnout, and being a part of my school's character team and Hope Institute and seeing the changes that character education was making in my school, not only for students but for the staff, reinvigorated my reasons for why I became an educator. I tell people who ask me about character education that I would much rather be known as a teacher of character and being a key part of shaping a student of character than being known for the subjects I teach. Character is what makes us who we are and shapes our lives.

Authority for Leadership

Another lens which helps us understand the role of leaders in a school devoted to character development is the distinction sociologists make between "authority" and "power" in leadership.[20] Here the concept of authority takes us back to the original meaning of the word, "to create, enlarge or build." It's easy to overlook that the word "authority" combines "author" with "ity." "Power" by contrast is the force of law; command and control.

Those who lead by "authority" are servant leaders. Their appeal is in the strength of their characters, the power of their vision, and the attraction of their example, not in law and enforcement. Mother Teresa and Martin Luther King led from authority; so did Jesus of Nazareth and Abraham Lincoln. The Taliban and ISIS lead from power. Leaders in schools whose mission includes developing moral goodness in students need to lead from authority which is sustained by the strength of the school's Basic Beliefs.

Principals and teachers, as servant leaders, should be "authors". They are in the process of forming and shaping the souls and moral compasses of human beings, not merely teaching brains on a stick. In every hour of every class the teacher is an author in helping to shape something priceless with eternal significance in lives that count for good.

Transformational leadership proceeds from authority and builds a flourishing organization with a minimum of law or bureaucracy. The ideal of any community based on servant leadership, including schools, is "external freedom, inner control," few rules, strong character.

Level 5 Leadership

Jim Collins wrote a best-selling book on great businesses, *Good to Great*. Chapter 2, "Level 5 Leadership," was reprinted in the Harvard Business Review and became one of the Review's most popular articles. Collins created a leadership hierarchy and called the highest level, "Level 5 Leadership." Level 5 leaders are "self-effacing, quiet, reserved . . . a paradoxical blend of personal humility and professional will." Such leaders, Collins found, were at the helm as companies were transformed from "good to great."

Whether we are talking about school principals, assistant principals, classroom teachers, custodians or bus drivers, all are leaders, and student character will flourish as they lead as Level 5 Leaders; servant leaders, humble but devoted to the Basic Beliefs and highly determined. Such is the example everyone would want for students – nothing fancy but humility and a strong will for excellence. When such educators and workers are given a culture based on a noble mission and worthy core values, they will help produce students with excellent academic capability plus lives that count for good, something priceless.

So we have several prisms through which we can view school leadership: transactional/transformational; authority/power; and Level 5. They all bring us to the same conclusion. Leadership, which is part of a culture that yields strong and good character in students, thrives in a free environment in which students choose and do the good, not because they are ordered, but because they are affirmed by the teachers' delight in them and doing the right thing is nurtured by positive feelings.

Dr. Thomas Casteel, Principal, Harlan Elementary School: The "Harlan Way" is part of everyday conversations by adults and kids alike. "Are you showing the Harlan Way?" We talk about the traits in our announcements, in character lessons, and students receive Praise Referrals by any adult in the building who sees them exhibiting one of our character traits. Our data notebooks also have a section dedicated to character. Recently, a student shared with me a desire to recognize two other students she has noticed exemplifying one of the traits. When we need to speak with a student about discipline (which has decreased dramatically by the way), we talk to them about why their actions did or did not show the Harlan Way. Students are able to explain why they did not did not show integrity, responsibility, or whichever particular trait might have been involved. It is this real life-in the moment-teaching and learning that I think has evolved rather than a box to check to say we "did character ed".

Heaven or Hell

Grant Gilmore, formerly a law professor at Yale, a preeminent authority in the law of commercial "transactions," but also a philosopher of law, drew a stark contrast between leadership by "authority" and "power." "The worse the society the more law there will be. In heaven there will be no law and the lion will lie down with the lamb. In hell there will be nothing but law and it will be meticulously observed."[21]

This insight provides another lens through which we can think more deeply about servant leadership and culture in schools. If a school society operates in the transactional dimension alone, there is a need for laws, protocols, reports and discipline. And there will be exhaustion and burnout. This has been a significant issue in the charter school movement where there has been a heavy emphasis on the transactional. The more a school's society can develop a strong transformational dimension, the more the authority of the Basic Beliefs can begin to govern through virtue apart from law.

Where school activity is guided by a mission that includes character development and core values that inspire and empower students to live in a way that counts for good, that school will excel in the transactional dimension – there will be higher academic achievement – and also in the transformational dimension there will be greater satisfaction for teachers, pride in the school for students and their families, and joy for all.

The challenge of every school that undertakes a character initiative is to motivate students to abide in the school's culture. Some students may do so because of outside pressure. Others, hopefully most, will be motivated from within. Virtue cannot be commanded. It needs to proceed from desires in students' hearts and to bloom in their souls. Embracing virtue must "feel" good to the student. How teachers motivate the recalcitrant student is an art. It takes place in the emotional chamber of the student's soul which can be locked shut from within. Only the student can open it.

Dr. James K.A. Smith, whom we discuss in Chapter 6, calls this challenge that of the "recalibration" of loves or desires. We must keep in mind that loves cannot be required but must be coaxed. Loves are not mercenary. Rewards must be internal; in the students' hearts.

The teacher must be aware that he or she is an "author" in the process of working to create something of priceless value in the hearts and souls of students.

Only One Life

Warren Buffett, the business icon, compares the human soul to a college graduate's receiving the gift of a new car, pristine and fully equipped, but with the admonition that this is the only car the graduate will ever own. How then will the graduate care for the car? The thought process this question evokes applies to students. Each student has only one life, one soul. What will become of that life and soul depends in large part on the character developed in the K-12 years.

Whether educators are in pre-school programs, kindergartens, elementary, middle or high schools, they are teaching fearfully and wonderfully made children or young adults who have but one life and need not only well educated minds but souls whose minds, motivations and wills are aligned to guide them on the path of lives that count for good. We discuss this essential point more fully in Chapter 5. The cultures of schools will have a significant input on the students' lives following the K-12 years. The Hope Institute believes that preparing and maintaining these cultures is of the highest importance in every school.

We are all Imitators

In considering the importance of culture in character formation, we need to understand that "teaching" virtues grows in large part from the example of mentors with whom there is loving interaction. The "authority" we discussed above comes from the power of example of the leader as a servant devoted to students. Hypocrites have no authority. They depend on law and punishment. And, of course, the example of leaders, principals, teachers and staff must exhibit the precepts of the Basic Beliefs. If, for instance, a core value of a school is "honesty" students will embody honesty more from the integrity they see in teachers than text book instruction. Aristotle, long ago, observed that "Imitation is . . . natural from childhood; humans are the most imitative creatures in the world and learn first by imitation."[22]

The great African-American novelist, James Baldwin, got to the heart of the matter when he reflected: "Children have never been very good at listening to their elders, but they have never failed to imitate them."[23] And the English political philosopher, Edmund Burke, summed it up: "Example is the school of mankind. It will learn at no other." [24]

And, of course, students will tend to find the easiest way when they can. Students, as imitators, will observe the weaknesses of their mentors and, when they are easier, practice them, forming bad habits, which will be instrumental in their character formation. What school leaders preach, they must practice and remember that actions speak louder than words.

Freedom

It is often said that character is "what you do when no one is looking." That's not a definition used in this book, but it gets to an important point about character – when students do the right thing when no one is looking, they do it because it has become second nature to them, part of their characters. They do it even when there are no observers to shame or police or enforcers to punish; they do it freely.

We need to note we are talking about freedom to do the "right thing" not do anything. The ethic of virtue sees freedom as free to do as students ought, not free to do whatever they want. The Basic Beliefs provide boundaries. So do virtues. If a student agrees that "honesty" is a virtue, the goal will be that honesty become second nature so the student is no longer "free" to be dishonest. Freedom requires virtue, and virtues have boundaries.

School cultures need to motivate students to live responsibly in freedom, apart from law, guided by the restraints of virtue. Without virtue, freedom is not possible, and virtue will not develop apart from a culture that nourishes freedom. Our nation's forefathers were keenly aware of this.

When our founders created a democratic republic, where ultimate sovereignty was in free people, not a king, an interest in virtue was reborn. Edmund Burke, an Englishman and student of the American experiment, wrote, "Society cannot exist unless a controlling power upon will and appetite be placed somewhere and the less there is within [virtue] the more there must be without [law, police and punishment]." This is true of schools' governments or, in fact, any organization. All of the nation's founders agreed that if freedom was given the people and government was placed in their hands, without virtue the American government would fail.[25] "Virtue . . . is a necessary spring of popular government," said President Washington. His successor, John Adams, added, "Only a virtuous people are capable of freedom." The third President, Thomas Jefferson, agreed, "The order of nature [is] that . . . happiness is inseparable from the practice of virtue." President Madison followed, "To suppose that any form of government will secure liberty or happiness without virtue is a chimerical idea."[26] [27] [28] A generation later the Frenchman, Alexis de Tocqueville, a keen observer of American culture, ascribed the greatness of the experiment in democracy to "habits of the heart."[29]

Of course, moving a school culture from law and regulation to freedom does not cost many dollars, but it must follow the adoption of Basic Beliefs, the embracing of them first by school leaders and then by the entire school community.

We can look around at families, companies, sports teams, governments – wherever we find free people doing great things – we will find a culture based in freedom that nurtures success and happiness. As President Jefferson observed, it is an "order of nature." And this order is fully applicable in K-12 schools. If in their schools leaders want success – learning, good test scores and the delight of teachers and students alike – the first task is to create a culture built around a worthy mission and time-honored values, and let it produce virtue and from virtue an abundant harvest. That harvest will be priceless.

CHAPTER 5

SOUL AND HEART

A school's academic program is mostly about teaching the mind. The teacher uses books and instructs students in reading, writing, math, geography, etc. in lower grades and more advanced courses as the student progresses.

Character development has a broader and different focus. It involves the human soul. In schools it is about equipping students with souls to live successful and morally good lives.

The Hope Academy will provide much instruction and opportunity for reflection on school programs and teaching practices that will lead to good and strong characters. Dr. Lickona's excellent book, *Character Matters*, has a thorough discussion of these practices.

But how is character formed in the soul of a student? Teachers know how to teach the moral precepts. But how can the student be motivated to desire to do the right thing and thereby grow in character to pursue a life that counts for good? As noted in Chapter 4, the latch to the student's soul is locked from within. The motivation freely to pursue the virtuous life must come from within. This chapter will provide one view of how students' souls choose to pursue a life that counts for good.

The Human Soul

So what do we mean when we use the word, "soul?" It is useful in analysis to understand the student's soul as having three functional parts – the mind, the emotions (affections, loves, desires, feelings, etc.) and the will. From time immemorial there has been a problem of conflict within the human soul,[30] and the same conflict is at play in every student's soul. The student's mind and conscience, from teaching, example and culture, may discern what is morally good but the student's desires too often want to take another path. When this happens, within the student's soul there is a conflict between the mind on the one hand and the desires or motivations on the other. The student's will must choose. If the will is weak, then selfish and fun-seeking emotions can override the mind and the student will choose the wrong thing.

Between selfish or lustful desires and feelings on the one hand and the mind on the other, desires and feelings win most every time. Cardinal Newman, an English Catholic Bishop, keenly observed, "Moor a battleship with thread or quarry granite with a razor blade, such is easier than controlling the pride and passion of man with the mind."[31]

Let's look at two examples, one seemingly trivial and one that involves destiny. For most students, when the alarm clock went off this morning, their mind understood it was time to start the day. But their feelings signaled it easiest to turn over and go back to sleep. "What's wrong with being a few minutes late?" they likely pondered. Whether to get up and start the day on time will be decided by the will – and students will have dozens of similar occasions in the day, whether: to smile and say "good morning;" to yawn or slouch in a class; to slant the truth a little when no one knows the difference; to make fun of a weak co-student; to open up the cell phone to a porn site; to encourage a despondent friend who has a sick parent; to offer solace to a lonely fellow student rejected by the crowd.

If we move to destiny-making decisions our students make as they mature, there is the myth of "The Choice of Hercules."[32] It is said that Hercules in his life's travels came to a fork in the road. Each road beyond the fork was attended by an angel. One road was marked, "Vice" and here a nymph promised a life of endless pleasure and ease, one of expanding wealth, comfort, good food, wine and lustful delights. No mention was made of the emptiness or regrets that were likely found along and at the end of the road. The other fork was marked, "Virtue" and here the attending angel spoke of responsibility and hard work, facing problems, overcoming losses, confronting dangers but forgetting self and pursuing worthy causes. The angel advised that along the road there would be seasons of satisfaction and the destination would bring happiness and contentment of a life well lived. Of course, students' minds might understand that the road of "virtue" was the one to take, but feelings, focused on ease and many pleasures would urge that they take the path of vice (at least for a little while their feelings might urge). What will their *will* decide? More to the point, how might schools prepare students for such a decision or a series of similar decisions that come bit by bit – for these are the form of moral decisions that each student will make and bit by bit they will determine the students' character and destiny.

It is the job of parents, teachers, religious leaders, coaches and mentors to teach, train and motivate the affections and wills of students to desire and choose the path of virtue; to choose virtue and its related trials, denials, accomplishments and internal rewards over immediate pleasure and ease.

In schools that choose to focus on character development, students will learn about the promises of the road of virtue – for it is on the road of virtue that most of the good in this world will be found: the material advancements, the commercial inventions, the medical and scientific inno-vations, the hospitals, soup kitchens, best schools, churches or synagogues, the arts, the happy marriages, selfless giving, all true happiness but much hard work and delayed gratification. Teachers want students to live and thrive in such a world in roles suitable for them. Having the will to choose the road of virtue, to pursue a life that counts for good even when it requires sacrifice, is the morally good way, and our students can walk this path only if virtues are planted in their souls through practice and begin to develop in them when they are young.

Let us turn now to a brief look at the three faculties of students' souls and how virtues are critical to their moral development.

The Mind

The mind is primary as everything students learn, their thoughts, rea-soning and what they see, hear and touch, comes through the mind. The first moral obligation is to think clearly.[33] But the mind, standing alone, is weak. Even when students seek to think clearly, they can be deceived or overcome by lies or by ambition, anger, greed, envy, pride, lust or other passions and vices. Students' minds need the support of their wills for good intentions to be carried into action, and their wills need the strength and stability of the virtues to choose the right thing and to stick with it.

The Emotions or Affections

The emotions are in the chamber of the soul where our students' desires, affections and passions (good and bad) reside. We use "affections" herein in the sense of strong desires that induce the will to fully engage. The affec-tions fortify the will. Affections in pursuit of a worthy purpose are what drive progress in our world and are good. Selfish affections for the wrong thing like drugs, power, wealth, sex or porn can be destructive and are at war with what the mind knows is good. The power of a student's soul for good is in the drive of affections through virtue.

The Will

The will is the executive center of the student's soul.[34] It organizes human life. It chooses or refuses everything students consciously do. It has been said, and properly so, that it is the whole person active. A student's mind can know what is right but be resisted by worldly passions and the will is needed to overcome destructive passions and carry the right thing into action.

The student's will does not operate alone. It needs the mind to know the truth. It draws strength from good affections and the virtues. Without this strength, the student's will can be overridden by feelings arising in the moment. Feelings, as impulses, can be dangerous if the will is not anchored in the virtues. Dr. Dallas Willard, formerly Dean of the Philosophy Department at the University of Southern California, writes, "A great part of the disaster of contemporary life lies in the fact that it is organized around feelings. [Students] nearly always follow their feelings.... The will is then left at the mercy of circumstances that evoke feelings."[35] Virtues (remember virtues are strengths), including practical wisdom, need to be implanted and developed by practice in students to become habits for the mind to discern what is good and the will to choose to do it whatever the circumstances. This process is rooted in culture more than classroom teaching. Likely, it can be carried out only in a strong culture, which can be supplemented in the classroom.

To sum it up, within students' souls are mind, emotions and will. The mind is where all morality begins, and it must be illumined. But, alone, it is weak compared to passions. The will is the executive center of the soul, and it must be empowered by affections and by virtues formed in a strong and good culture to tame expansive desires which would cause bad choices. For students, the mind needs to think clearly, good loves need to be cultivated and strengthened and virtues need to be formed so that the will can choose and walk the road to true happiness.

When students' minds, desires and wills are integrated to count for good, we find truly happy students, and such students will enjoy an "ordered soul" and a happy life.

It is obvious that for character formation the school must go beyond its traditional teaching role so that students' knowledge of the good will not be compromised by the power of vices. Through the school's culture, not classroom instruction alone, school leaders need to make every effort to guide students to love the good and to find joy in seeking it over the alluring and destructive pleasures offered by the vices. Students' souls need to be edified to know, treasure and make a difference for the good.

The Chest

C. S. Lewis, the Cambridge University professor, gave three lectures in 1946 criticizing an English school textbook that advocated a version of what was called "values clarification." Though education has moved away from values clarification, Lewis' graphic insights are helpful in understanding the working of the human soul.

His main point was that without virtue all we have in the soul are the mind and acquisitive appetites without any moral compass. He taught, "The head [should] rule the belly through the chest," (the "belly" being the insatiable appetite for more and the "chest" being stable dispositions or virtues.) He concluded, "In a sort of ghastly simplification we remove the organ [virtue] and demand the function. We make men without chests and expect of them virtue and enterprise. We laugh at honor and we are shocked to find traitors in our midst. We castrate and bid the gelding be fruitful."[36]

Lewis' urges that the mind and emotions, without virtue, will result in moral chaos. Morality must have a stabilizing factor, a moral compass which checks appetites so students can be fruitful.

Students' souls have minds and emotions, but the will trained by good habits and empowered by good loves is essential to any morally good life. If schools pay attention only to the mind, and neither within the school nor without is anyone paying attention to character, we will have "men without chests and expect of them virtue and enterprise," but instead find "traitors in our midst."

The Heart

Students of the inner workings of the human psyché acknowledge there is no precise delineation between soul and heart. The heart is the epicenter of the human person and the deeper desires and longings of the soul are concentrated in the heart. Thus, we have the teaching "where your treasure is, there your heart will be also."[37] If teachers want to know the heart of a student, the task is to find his or her deepest desires and loves and there teachers will find the heart.

The heart has a special place in the Judeo-Christian tradition. Hebrew wisdom teaches: "Above all else guard your heart, everything you do flows from it."[38] Whether one is religious or not, this concept is central to any character initiative.

The heart of young students needs to be guarded because it is vulnerable and has no armor or weapons to defend itself. It is easily wounded and readily deceived. In it are the student's loves, but there are forces about that will disorder loves and turn them away from worthy pursuits to things like popularity, drugs or porn, or turn them inward to corrosive self-love or suffocate them in laziness.

From the loves of students' hearts flow "everything [they] do." Their loves profoundly influence the choices of their wills.

Schools need to help students guard their hearts from deceit and destructive loves through providing a culture immersed in virtue. When students pursue worthy causes that transcend selfish interests and desires, the heart remains healthy and loves can be properly ordered with the mind, emotions and will integrated. A school's culture is needed to protect the hearts of the meek from bullying which most fundamentally is aimed at the heart of the vulnerable to gratify the ego of the strong.

It was Alexis de Tocqueville who coined the phrase "habits of the heart" in *Democracy in America* (1835). "Habits of the heart," a good synonym for "virtues," are virtuous habits that grow from and are nourished by the treasures of the heart. Take the "heart" out of moral choices and if students are to do the right thing, they must fall back on "duty," a choice of the will apart from affections of the heart. There is a noble place for duty in the ethical life. It works well in the military, is useful in scouting, and in schools is a way-station to virtue; but duty as a destination makes for a dreary school.

C. S. Lewis, always provocative, captures the limitations of "duty" in ethical living:

> "A perfect man would never act from a sense of duty; he'd always want the right thing more than the wrong one. Duty is only a substitute for love (of God and of other people) like a crutch which is a substitute for a leg. Most of us need the crutch at times; but of course it is idiotic to use the crutch when our own legs (our own loves, tastes, habits, etc.) can do the journey on their own."[39]

Virtue, a habit of the heart, leads to students' delights. We all need duty (plus grit) some of the time to act responsibly. But virtue is more to be desired.

So understood character education should acquaint the head with the long-term satisfaction and happiness that one finds in a life of virtue. But educators should remember that character development is not behavior modification through rules and enforcement, which emphasize duty. It is inward transformation of the soul through affections and virtues formed in a strong, relational culture. Through personal relationships, example and practice, teachers and mentors need to help cultivate the affections of a student to love a life which counts for good. Our next chapter will turn to love as a virtue, the overarching virtue which grows in relationships.

CHAPTER 6

LOVE

Love is the Preeminent Virtue

School leadership needs to carefully consider whether to make love the driving force of any successful school character initiative. The simple reason is that love, properly understood, is the preeminent virtue. This is not a religious statement though those in the Judeo-Christian tradition would agree as in both the Hebrew and Christian sacred texts love of neighbor is a central focus. The apostle Paul wrote love is the "greatest" virtue and admonished all to "pursue love."[40] But atheists also agree. André Comte-Sponville, an atheist and leading ethics philosopher at the Sorbonne in Paris, writes that "love is the alpha and omega of all virtue."[41] We might add that Victor Frankl, a Holocaust survivor, and one of the leading psychiatrists of the 20th Century, declared that love was the "highest and greatest good to which man can aspire."[42] And in the world of character in schools, Dr. Tom Lickona refers to love as "the most powerful force in the universe."[43]

As for schools, there is the fundamental principle attributed to Dr. King that "whom you would transform, you must first love."[44] Relationships can be created by law and contracts are enforceable by courts, but in a culture that will engender virtue – a culture based on freedom as in schools – love needs to be the source of relationships. A student's life is transformed in loving relationships and a community founded on virtue. Only through relationships can good character be formed in students. And such formation occurs one student and one soul at a time.

What then is the love we are talking about? The English language, unlike others, has a single word for love. A student might love hot dogs and God, expressed with the same word. And the single word, love, covers the whole panoply of desires, of romantic attachment, caring within the family, sacrificial devotion and more. Can schools find a single concept that unifies all of these loves? Perhaps one concept can be used for most loves at the entry level and that is "delight" or approval in the existence of another person or thing. Students may delight in hot dogs, parents, siblings or other students. Delight is a great sentiment for every human relationship and encounter in schools.

Teacher and Student

What is the love a teacher should have for students? It begins with delight in each and every student as a human being, "fearfully and wonderfully made" to quote Hebrew wisdom. For each student, the teacher's mindset should be, "it is good that you exist." There are no "ordinary" students. The teacher should see the student's soul as a precious work in process every hour of every day and on that truth relationally move beyond the transactional mode (for the sake of the system, I must prepare the student to score well on a test) to the transformational (in light of the school's Basic Beliefs, for the sake of the student, I want to help every student achieve his or her fullest potential in head and heart). Only with this attitude in the heart of the teacher can the teacher form a relationship with a student and from this relationship play a significant role in a student's character development. This is true whether or not the word "love" appears in the Basic Beliefs. With this attitude, a world of creativity, resourcefulness and joy opens up.

From delight there grows a relationship which is the soil that nurtures love.

Liz Huntley[45] is one of Alabama's leading courtroom lawyers, a trustee of Auburn University and President of The Hope Institute. At age 5 Liz's mother had committed suicide, her father, a drug dealer, was absent or in prison, and she lived as a foster child with her grandmother in a government project in Clanton, Alabama, many miles from her Huntsville home. First, in a church pre-school program and then in the first grade, there were teachers who delighted in Liz, treated her as special, loved her and prepared the way for Liz to live into her potential. In cultures of delight and love, Liz blossomed and learned to love reading and making A's in school.

At age five Liz was without parents but as a child was a unique young woman with enormous potential. She needed an education but even more she needed the encouraging love of adults if she was to grow into her potential.

Now with one daughter at Vanderbilt and another as president of the Auburn University student body, Liz fondly remembers her first grade teacher, Ms. Jones, who had a sincere delight in Liz's wellbeing and was a vital key in the success Liz has found. Forty years later Liz and Ms. Jones remain devoted to each other.

Relationships, teacher and student, begin with courtesy. Names are learned, eye contact is made, delight is expressed as a courtesy. From basic courtesy the seed of a relationship can be planted and begin to grow. And this relationship can be the beginning of priceless transformation – "whom you would transform you must first love."

The story of Teddy Stoddard[46] portrays one of the myriad of ways a teacher-student relationship can grow into something priceless. Teddy was assigned to Ms. Robinson's fifth grade class. He was a sullen boy, dirty clothes and no friends. Ms. Robinson reacted negatively, gave him bad grades and waited for the opportunity to pass him on to the next teacher. But Ms. Robinson learned a few things about Teddy. He was a bright child and in the third grade his mother had died and since his father had ignored him. Ms. Robinson regretted that she had turned a cold shoulder, and when the class shared Christmas presents, Teddy's gift to Ms. Robinson was a half-empty bottle of cheap perfume, something left behind when his mother died. Ms. Robinson, now ashamed, put a few drops on her wrist. Teddy spoke to her after class, "Ms. Robinson, you smell just like my mom used to."

A relationship was born and as the story goes, Ms. Robinson's life as a teacher changed. "On that very day, she quit teaching reading and writing and arithmetic. Instead she began teaching children." She began to pay special attention to Teddy and twenty years later he graduated from medical school. His father had died, and when Teddy married, he saved a place for Ms. Robinson as "mother of the groom."

Some say this story is fiction, but it teaches pure truth – from very little things teacher-student relationships grow into a form of love which transforms both teacher and student. No cost, no books, just love.

Dr. Marvin Berkowitz, McDonnel Professor of Education, Director of the Center for Character and Citizenship and University Professor, all at the University of Missouri-St. Louis, and a national authority on character in schools, is especially interested in the problem student whom he calls a "Tarnished Child." Dr. Berkowitz uses a catchy title for his book, *You Can't Teach Through a Rat*, to write a marvelous text on (among much more) the relationship of teacher to student, based on love. He observes, "For a Tarnished Child a teacher's love and interest in them can make all the difference in the world. These children have not known such a relationship and typically don't believe they could ever be the object of an adult's unqualified and healthy love."[47]

The only way a student – or anyone – can know love is to receive it. Students love when they are first loved. Knowledge of love is not like knowledge of an automobile or an oak tree which can be seen and touched. Love, to be known, must be given from one human to another and received in the heart. And scientists are agreed that students yearn for and must receive love from adults to have healthy souls. A research report joined by thirty-three scientists entitled *Hardwired to Connect* concluded that all children need authoritative communities devoted to transmitting a model of the moral life. On the basis of research, the scientists concluded that children or students are "hardwired" to need loving connections and moral guidance. [48] If a child does not receive love at home, a school through its culture and teachers may be the last resort. And Dr. Berkowitz cautions teachers, "You matter …most of all to the 'Tarnished Children' who "can't live, sometimes literally, without you."[49]

Student and Student

Delight or approval should also be the attitude of all students for one another. Delight, not just for the talented, popular or good looking, but for every co-student, even those with special needs, or the awkward and rejected.

The Golden Rule provides the sublime value for students. (Though the Golden Rule might be discarded in some schools as "spiritual," it is an ethical standard the world over and the words, "Golden Rule" nowhere appear in sacred scripture.)

This discussion in a class in a school in Skaneateles, New York, under-scores the vitality of the Golden Rule as a standard for students in schools:

"Gary Robinson taught fourth and sixth graders in the Ska-neateles School District, Skaneateles, New York. On the first day of school he would ask his students, 'How would you like to be treated in this class – by me, the teacher, and by everyone else in the room? Write down to or three ways you'd like to be treated.'

"Students wrote that they wanted to be treated fairly, with respect, not made fun of or embarrassed, not left out, and so on. Mr. Robinson had them share their lists with a partner and discuss them as a class.

"He then asked a second question. "How should you treat everyone else in the room?" Students could see it logically fol-lowed if they wanted to be treated with respect and fairness, then that's exactly how they should treat everyone else. Mr. Robinson enlarged upon this point for the class:

"Every right carries a responsibility. If you've got a right to respect, then you've got a responsibility to extend that same respect to other people. You can't claim a right unless you accept the responsibility. They are two sides of the same coin.

"He summarized, 'We're saying you should treat others as you wish to be treated. Does anyone know what that's called?' Some-body in the class usually knew: 'the Golden Rule.'

"That's my main classroom rule," Mr. Robinson said. Then he unfurled a large banner with these words writ large: TREAT OTHERS AS YOU WISH TO BE TREATED. He hung the banner above the blackboard, where it remained for the rest of the year."[50]

Notice there is no mention of "love," but the virtue of love is wrapped in the Golden Rule. Habits of love will be formed in Mr. Robinson's classes which, when supplemented by other teachers, will bring joy to students for a lifetime.

Prioritizing Loves

Professor James K.A. Smith has written a book entitled, *You Are What You Love*. Its theme is that what students love or treasure will determine their characters. Students can love all sorts of things, including God, but the students' treasures need to be prioritized in their souls.

Augustine, a 5th Century Christian philosopher, summarized this critical idea in five very important words: "Virtue is love rightly ordered."[51] Educators need to think through this remarkable insight. If it is true, then all virtue is tied to love or many loves, and certainly love is the preeminent virtue. Students need to rank their loves. If Augustine is correct, virtue is none other than loving the right things in the right order and doing what love motivates. From love manifested in action grows a life that counts for good, something The Hope Institute thinks is priceless. Therefore, the overarching purpose of a school's Basic Beliefs and how they are lived out in the school's culture is helping students love the right things.

Healthy loves, which empower students to count for good, need to be refreshed continuously and strengthened such as love for God (if the student is religious); love for parents and family; love for others including those of different ethnic or national backgrounds, rich and poor, beautiful or not; love for learning; love for the truth, etc. Other more neutral loves need to be subordinated and limited such as love for snack foods, social media, sports, TV, even golf, etc. And other loves, which impede a life that counts for good, need to be stifled altogether like love for narcotic drugs, porn and bullying. We can add to the lists. The student's will based on the mind's understanding and strengthened by virtue formed in good cultures must prioritize loves. Quite simply, the worth and excellence of a soul is measured by the object of its loves and deeds. The true character of every student, and every teacher, is found in his or her loves.

Love is a Verb and Can be Tough

There are some who dismiss love as a virtue by demoting it to a feeling. There is a "feeling" dimension to love, but love is most fundamentally a verb, something people do. Consider Stephen R. Covey's discussion in his *Seven Habits of Highly Successful People*:

> In the great literature of all progressive societies, love is a verb. Reactive people make it a feeling. . . . Proactive people make love a verb. *Love is something you do*: sacrifices you make, the giving of self like a mother bringing a newborn into the world. If you want to study love, study those who sacrifice for others. . . .(emphasis added) [52]

Who are the proactive people? Dr. Martin Luther King, Mother Teresa, Mahatma Gandhi, and Jesus of Nazareth, to name a few. For all of these love was a verb. They are admired for what they did. In schools love is something teachers choose with their wills to do as affections for a "fearfully and wonderfully made" student are formed.

Some, especially on the masculine side, may be inclined to dismiss love as a vital part of a school's culture because they consider it too sweet, soft or malleable. Love can be kind and gentle. But love is the alpha and omega of all virtues. Love is wise, courageous, protective of all, especially the weak or unpopular. Love is gritty; it perseveres. It is a virtue that includes both milk (structure and firmness) and honey (kindness). Love can pack power or be tender. A teacher's love can be expressed as kindness when it enables a student's success or good habits. Love is never expressed in kindness that enables bad habits. Where there is a bad habit, love wants it gone, even when it hurts. To protect the integrity of a school's Basic Beliefs or the welfare of other students, love can reprimand, discipline and ultimately, as a last resort, expel. Love's nature is to subordinate self and attend to the legitimate needs of others (essentially the meaning of virtue) which can require gentleness or toughness.

It will be up to the leadership in each school whether to make love explicit in its Basic Beliefs. Many leaders will find the word subject to misunderstanding and may turn to a partial synonym like empathy, compassion or caring, which is okay. But as the power of love, however named, becomes a central part of a school's culture, it will release great energy, accomplishment and delight in the school.

Hal Urban, a national authority on character in schools, concludes his best-selling book, *Life's Greatest Lessons*, with the thought that by "being good" we enjoy "emotional and spiritual health."[53] He is right, and "being good" is a substitute for "love." When it comes to skills, being good is not the highest compliment. For skills or ability, we might use "excellent," "great," or "phenomenal" as the highest accolade. For morals or virtue, "being good" is what teachers should strive for. It is what every school should seek for its students. Of course, in the world of morals, no one is "good" without love.

In the realm of character, the two are inseparable and both give our students "emotional and spiritual health."

Love in Sports

Love by whatever name creates teamwork and success. Coach Dabo

Swinney credited love as the catalyst for Clemson's 2017 football national championship. The University of Virginia's 2018 basketball national championship team was built around belief in the power of "Family," a community united by love. Coach Vince Lombardi, one of the toughest and most successful head coaches in the National Football League's history, commented that his accomplishments were coupled with his love for his players. Love can be tough. And Coach Lombardi agreed with Emerson, "Character is higher than intellect."[54]

Joe Ehrmann was an All American defensive tackle at Syracuse University and played for thirteen years in the NFL for the Baltimore Colts and the Detroit Lions. He was a tough guy. His father was a professional boxer and a stevedore. After pro football, as part of an inner-city ministry, Ehrmann worked closely with the Gilman Greyhounds, a high school football team in Baltimore which was perennially one of the best teams in the northeast. He cared about teaching young men two things – nurturing relationships and living for a cause (a "life that counts for good"). He told them that ultimately wins and losses are not the most important thing (Gilman was undefeated several seasons), but the really important things in life were building strong relationships especially in the family and living for a transcendent cause. Here was Ehrmann's exchange with the team before games:

> Ehrmann: "What is our job as coaches?"
>
> Players: "To love us."
>
> Ehrmann: "What is your job?"
>
> Players: "To love each other."

Ehrmann used football to develop relationships with boys in high school to teach them to be men and to love one another.[55]

Love and Happiness

It has been said that all true happiness is fundamentally the happiness of love.[56] Teachers, principals and staff might think about and discuss this proposition. They might ask themselves whether the happiest moments of their professional lives were not when they made a student happy by delighting in the student and helping the student become "smart and good," the essential purposes of schools.

The happiness of love is a critical facet of every successful school character initiative. We can recall Thomas Jefferson's remark: "Happiness is inseparable from the practice of virtue." Think about this. Is he right? The road of virtue (see Hercules Choice, Chapter 5) is where true happiness is found and not in the short-term escapades that ensnare so many students. As the Danish philosopher, Soren Kierkegaard, put it, "the one who sets his heart on pleasure, has set his foot on the road to despair."[57] Pleasure is fine and enjoyable, but students best not set their hearts on it. Virtue, and specifically love, has its recompense in the deepest happiness known to humankind.

Love from teacher to student opens up the world of virtue for the student and fills the teacher's heart with joy. Love, student to student, if it is no more than delight one for the other, is where their true happiness in school begins.

In summing up how to be an effective teacher, Dr. Berkowitz writes, "First, love kids. Glory in them.... Find out what is fun and joyous about kids. . . And let the love shine."[58] What more need be said? Let the love shine! Dr. Berkowitz has been a tremendous help to The Hope Institute and challenges all our Academy classes.

The virtue of love unleashes the full potential of any school. If love, by its own name or any other, is at the heart of a school's Basic Beliefs, all activity growing from those beliefs will cause the school to flourish: learning will improve; students' characters will strengthen; and the school has the potential to become a joy and delight to all. All this is priceless!

CHAPTER 7

THE BIG PICTURE

This book has concentrated on what virtue is; how it forms in students; how schools can develop cultures which influence its growth; and how character initiatives make schools stronger in all they do as they are strengthened by Basic Beliefs from which students grow in virtue.

This chapter takes the discussion broader and deeper and in an abbreviated way develops context beyond schools.

The ideas outlined hopefully will prompt thought and discussion about whether and how virtue is essential to fulfillment in every human life, school, neighborhood, city, state and nation. All goodness in life ultimately develops from virtue. This promise is the reason The Hope Institute exists.

The Cosmic Conflict

A contest between good and evil, virtue and vice, has been with humankind from the beginning. Every student will live in it. Some will find dignity, peace and happiness. Others will be buffeted about in a way that will bring anxiety and frustration.

Schools can make a difference in preparing students to flourish as they enter the fray.

First, here is an outline of some of the major factors that create disorder.

Scientists in their observation of the physical universe have arrived at the Second Law of Thermodynamics, a name for the conclusion that ever so slowly the universe is "running down" or "wasting away" and over billions of years the sun will grow cold and all matter will fall into an undifferentiated blob.

Moving to recent history, in the last century the United States fought in two world wars and in the Korean, Vietnam, Iraq and Afghanistan conflicts, in which millions were killed, cities were bombed and the earth scorched. There were genocides in the Soviet Union, Cambodia and Rwanda. Gun violence in America rose exponentially, especially in the larger cities.

All around human bodies are breaking down, aging, inevitably to die; diseases are taking their toll; commercial buildings are deserted and rotting away; so are factories, church and school buildings; junkyards are full of wrecked vehicles.

In the human realm, prisons are overflowing, suicides are increasing, cybercrime is rampart and addictions – alcohol, drugs, gambling, sex, money – are on the rise.

Scott Peck in his masterful book, *The Road Less Traveled*, calls the forces behind this deterioration the "forces of entropy,"[59] entropy being the final resting place of the Second Law of Thermodynamics.

We can recall the song the Kingston Trio made popular in the late '50s:

> They're rioting in Africa,
> they're starving in Spain,
> there's hurricanes in Florida
> and Texas needs rain.

> They're rioting in Africa,
> there's strife in Iran,
> what nature doesn't do to us
> will be done by our fellow man.

And the drift of many in the 1950s and '60s and perhaps now was and is to capitulate, give up and drop out.

But we cannot stop with the bad news. Dr. Peck turns our attention to counter-forces to the ravages of entropy, and they abound in nature and in human virtue.

In nature there is springtime every year and sunrise every morning. The sun warms and rains refresh. Over the millennia, divine providence and evolution have developed life from the smallest plants and creatures to the great rain forests and humans with DNA of amazing complexity and a frontal cortex capable of immense knowledge and amazing problem solving.

And we find the forces for goodness ascending. Dr. Berkowitz, one of the nation's foremost leaders in character education, quotes Dr. Martin Luther King: "The arc of the moral universe is long but it tends toward justice."[60] With morality the glass is more than half full though we still have miles and miles to go. It has taken almost 900 years to move from the Magna Carta (where the king of England ceded some of his power to the land-owning aristocracy) to where we are today in the United States in the quest that everyone be equally subject to the law and have equal opportunity under the law. We have the United States Constitution creating a democratic republic and its Bill of Rights. A deadly civil war and a great President, Abraham Lincoln, established freedom and citizenship for former slaves. We have the Fourteenth Amendment extending the protection of the Bill of Rights to all states and local governments and the Fifteenth Amendment prohibiting racial discrimination in voting. There is the Nineteenth Amendment giving women the right to vote.

Dr. Berkowitz draws on a legend in the Hebraic tradition that gives us the phrase, *Tikkun Olam*, meaning "heal the world."[61] Behind this concept is a legend that the world was somehow damaged in its creation and needs to be healed.

All about forces are healing a broken world. Dread diseases – malaria, polio, HIV – are cured. Clean water is more and more available in the developing world. Vaccines are developed in months to fight a pandemic. Agricultural, industrial and technical advances are lifting billions out of poverty and raising the standard of living for more billions across the globe. Transportation and communication are drawing us all together in work to heal the world.

One reason the "arc of the moral universe tends toward justice" is that ultimately the force of evil is on a fool's errand. Where evil appears most fierce and daunting, virtue springs to life to overcome it. When evil creates martyrs, warriors for justice are aroused. The Hebrew nation was formed following the persecution of Pharaoh. It is said that "the blood of martyrs is the seed of the church." The crucifixion of a Nazarene launched the Christian church. The early Christian writings encouraged believers to "rejoice in suffering" and count it "pure joy" when encountering persecutions and trials because suffering produces "mature and complete" people.[62] The evils of the English Star Chamber motivated the protections of the American Bill of Rights. Nazism aroused the virtue of America's greatest generation which in turn helped in building a stronger and united Europe.

Driving all forces for good in the human realm is the strength of virtue.

And undergirding and uniting all virtue is the power of love. Love and its panoply of virtues are the reason that the arc of the moral universe tends toward justice.

Dr. Peck observes that "love is the miraculous force that defies the natural law of entropy."[63] Can we agree? And quite logically Dr. Peck deduces that laziness is the chief of vices because laziness drains the responsibility birthed by human love to heal the world.[64] It is ultimately love that combats the vices within and the forces of entropy without. Humans become lazy because we want to avoid the strain, toil and suffering of love in the fight against vices and the forces of entropy.

As we look at virtue from this higher perspective, we will find that virtue has a role to play in institutions as well as individuals. In all institutions there is this cosmic conflict between the force of entropy and the strength of virtue. The institution itself must generate virtue if it is to overcome the force of entropy. This insight applies most especially to the institution of schools.

Institutions

Virtue is formed primarily in institutions, including schools. So, what is an institution?

Institutions have many functions and exist in a broad range from government agencies to families. They have three characteristics in common. First, they are communities. A single person is never an institution, nor does virtue grow in a single human apart from community. Dr. Hunter at the University of Virginia writes that "Character outside of a lived community, the entanglement of ... relationships and their shared story, is impossible."[65]   Second, institutions are durable – they exist over time because like schools and family they serve an essential purpose. Third, written or unwritten, they have a distinct mission and core values. For many institutions, the mission and values are stated in an oath, vow, pledge or creed. There is the marriage vow, the Boy Scout Oath, the Apostles' Creed. All members of Congress, state legislatures, all judges, members of the armed forces and law enforcement swear by oath to pursue a mission in accordance with core values.

The American Enterprise Institute is a public policy "think tank." Yuval Levin, a prolific author, is its Director of Cultural and Social Studies, and has written an incisive book, *A Time to Build*, which discusses the pivotal role of institutions in the formation of character.

He writes:

> [Those such as Levin who hold the traditional view of character believe] each of us is born deficient but capable of moral improvement . . . and this improvement – the formation of character and virtue – is the foremost work of our society in every generation. To fail to engage in it is to regress to pre-civilization barbarism. This work is the traditional, defining purpose of our institutions, which must, therefore be fundamentally formative.[66]

We need to reflect on these observations. They are stunning but true. First, the traditional view of character starts with the belief that humans are "born deficient."   Such a belief is too skeptical for many. It is fundamental to the Judeo-Christian world-view, the voice of the Hebrew prophets and most especially the writings of the apostle Paul who relied on the prophets. Over time in the eighteenth and nineteenth centuries, however, some philosophers began to argue that humans were not born deficient but were born with an essentially good nature and corrupted by institutions and markets, such as the crown, the aristocracy, the church and the bourgeois marketplace. Get rid of the institutions and free markets, it was argued, and humans will flourish. The French and Communist revolutions were built on these philosophies and created the slaughter of millions of humans; and economically and socially were disasters.

Humans need virtue because they [we] are "crooked timber" writes David Brooks, a world-renowned columnist and author of *The Road to Character*.[67] Brooks observes that "The long road to character begins with an accurate understanding of our nature, and the core of that understanding is that we are flawed creatures. We have an innate tendency toward selfishness and overconfidence."[68]

Virtue gives the strength to overcome our tendency toward selfishness and the vices. If humans are not "crooked timber" and moral weakness expressed in the vices is not the tendency of all, there is no need for virtue.

Levin continues: "the formation of character and virtue [is] the foremost work of our society in every generation and the failure of institutions to engage in character formation is a path to 'pre-civilization barbarism.' "

These are strong words. The civilization we enjoy today in the United States – our freedom, rights, rule of law, civic associations, mutual respect and high standard of living – depends on the virtue of our citizens. The two are directly related. The stronger the virtue, the more civil and prosperous is the nation.

We saw in Chapter 4 that this country's founders were agreed that without virtue the democratic republic created in our Constitution would fail. Unlike the leaders of the French revolution, America's founders were keenly aware that humans were "born deficient" and built checks and balances in a Bill of Rights and our Constitution to harness the moral corruption to which all lawmakers are vulnerable and which developed so rapidly in France and the Soviet Union. Quite simply, the United States remains strong politically and economically only to the degree that our institutions, including families and schools, develop virtue.

Therefore, Levin puts character formation at the center of the work of institutions: "This work is the essential, defining purpose of our institutions which must, therefore, be fundamentally formative."

The question every school leader should ask is whether his or her school, as an institution, needs to be "fundamentally formative" of the virtues that empower a life that counts for good amidst this conflict between good and evil.

Schools, even while excelling at teaching and learning, are part of a larger context where the future and strength of this nation depends in material part on how well they form virtue in their students. Many may disparage or even ignore schools, but school leaders should never lose sight of the fact that schools are institutions entrusted with children, fearfully and wonderfully made for lives that count for good. Ultimately the influence of a good school extends to the whole community. Each school needs to become a beacon illuminating the riches of the virtuous life. The promise of a good school extends far beyond academics and school walls. Schools fight the forces of entropy with a culture of virtue.

> **Dr. Nita Carr, President, Cornerstone Schools:** When Cornerstone expanded with a long-term lease for Woodlawn Methodist classroom facilities, across the street were six dilapidated houses, once lovely homes but recently deserted by their former owners and left to become houses for the drug trade and prostitution. The houses, owned by financial institutions, which had foreclosed delinquent mortgage loans, were available at very low prices. Cornerstone bought the houses, tore them down and replaced them with soccer fields, planted with grass and fenced to protect them. A row of dilapidated, decaying structures was replaced with a lovely field for Cornerstone students and youngsters all over the neighborhood to use for recreation.

Indeed, in the United States, the first and still the greatest democratic republic, each school is a critical and integral part of a national aspiration that will determine whether our land will "long be bright with freedom's holy light."

Far Back at the Beginning

The ideas pursued in this chapter may be new to you as they were to me when I began to read more about character. But they are in fact ancient, going back 2600 years to ancient Greece.

In a criminal trial in Athens, Socrates, the most famous and perhaps the greatest teacher of all time, was charged with corrupting the morals of minors and sentenced to death. In his closing argument, Socrates asserted that his teaching to "younger" and "older" alike was that they should seek neither money nor survival ahead of caring for their "souls." He concluded, "Not from money does virtue come, but from virtue comes money and all other good things for human beings, both privately and publically."[69] Such is an eternal truth: *"from virtue comes all good things."*

Aristotle, one of the world's greatest philosophers, followed Socrates and first taught the *Ethics* in lectures in Athens which are the foundation of this book's teaching on virtue and character. He followed with the *Politics*, the first and greatest text on how communities should be organized and governed. The key to the *Politics* is that leaders must understand that the good life of citizens is more than survival and riches but rather consists in a life of virtuous activity.[70]

What Socrates and Aristotle teach (and it is just as true today as in their time) is that every student will be able to achieve their fullest human potential only through virtuous activity. There is indeed in every human soul a contest between the force of entropy and the strength of virtue, between vice and virtue. As the great Russian novelist and freedom fighter, Aleksander Solzhenitsyn, put it, "the battleline between good and evil runs through the heart"[71] of every human and every student.

No matter how fully and perfectly schools teach and train the human brain, the key to the fullness and happiness of every student life is in virtue and so is the quality of life in every town, city, county, state and school.

Herein lies the short and complete answer to the question, "what is a life that counts for good?" It is a life of virtuous activity. The Hope Institute believes it is something every school principal, staff member and teacher should aspire for every student.

CHAPTER 8

AND BEYOND

C haracter development is a long-term process. Good and strong character builds bit by bit over the long term in humans and what is begun can be lost if it is not refreshed and reenergized. It will take years to determine whether a student has developed strong character.

A Long Road

The mother of a boy playing high school football for the Gilmore Greyhounds, (see Chapter 6) attended a preseason scrimmage and asked the head coach how successful the boys were going to be. The coach responded, "We'll know in twenty years." The coach saw his job in the transformational dimension; the mother was focused on the transactional, wins and losses.

At the transactional level, tests can assess progress in a month or year. When thinking about character development, the measure is in terms of years or decades. The KIPP charter school program had a single objective in its initial mission – to get every student ready for college. It operated on the transactional plane and had spectacular success with grades and test scores, but soon enough KIPP learned that its students, though readily admitted to college, were dropping out. The academic progress could be easily assessed. But academic progress meant little if students did not have the character to persevere in college. The Gilman coach was correct. It would take decades before a verdict could be reached on character development.

What we learn from Liz Huntley's and Terry Stoddard's stories is that little things that foster loving interaction between a student and a teacher can have deep-rooted, lasting significance for a student which takes years to manifest fully. Schools and school boards must be patient about progress in student character.

> **Dr. Patricia Simpson, former Principal, Edgewood Elementary School:** It was the last hour of kindergarten for Patricia Simpson's first class of 15 kindergarten students. With a huge lump in her throat at the thought of being with the students for the last time, Mrs. Simpson told the children that she may not see them every day anymore; but, she would see them at their high school graduation. Although the students did not understand the significance of that statement, Mrs. Simpson did. Twelve years later, she attended the high school graduation of each student from her first kindergarten class. Although many of the students were still students in the same district, travel to a couple of states was necessary; the farthest was to a graduation in Pittsburgh, PA. Forty years later, many of those students and their kindergarten teacher still keep in contact. That's the love of a teacher.

But fortunately, as a school's leadership begins to focus on student character, and school culture enters the transformational phase, progress at the transactional level will be seen earlier. For those who think success should be measured in the transactional dimension alone – and many leaders, especially in public life do – there should be early indicators that a character initiative is bearing fruit in academic achievement.

And school leaders will find that most, though probably not all, teachers will become supporters. Most who choose to enter education as a profession do so to make a transforming difference in youngsters' lives. All too often and too soon they begin operating in the bureaucratic world of the transactional. They leave teaching, or if they remain, their ardor diminishes. When Basic Beliefs come to life, and they find leadership that empowers them to help in building character and transforming students' lives, they are ready to buy in and become supporters.

The "11 Principles"

If development in character is difficult to measure, how does school leadership determine if they are on track? The Hope Institute finds an excellent and comprehensive tool in Character.Org's *11 Principles of Effective Character Education*. Here is Character.Org's description of the "*11 Principles:*"

> "Based on decades of research on effective schools, the *11 Principles* serve as guideposts for schools to plan, implement, assess and sustain their comprehensive character development initiative.

> "Many school leaders also use the *11 Principles* as a school improvement process. The *11 Principles* focus on all aspects of school life, including school culture and climate, social and emotional learning (SEL), student engagement and academic achievement…teacher moral, and parent engagement."

Dr. Tom Lickona, a consultant to HI, is a primary author of the *11 Principles*. They provide an excellent and comprehensive guide to the many components of a character development initiative.

They are the foundation of the work of the HI.

They can be found at the Character.Org website.

We all know that the United States needs to improve its educational system. According to the *U. S. News and World Report*, the United States currently ranks about 30th in math and 10th in reading on a world-wide measure of national educational systems. And Alabama ranks 49th among the states of the United States.

Alabama's Department of Education and local boards are highly focused on the academic dimension of its schools. But we all know that smart students without good and strong character are not what any nation or state needs. Joseph Stalin, Adolph Hitler and Mao Zedong were very smart, but morally corrupt. As Theodore Roosevelt observed, "To educate a [student] in mind but not in morals is to educate a menace to society."[72] For our nation, state, town or county to achieve its potential, we need schools that produce both "smart and good" graduates. That would be good for our state and nation. It is essential for every fearfully and wonderfully created soul. It is priceless.

We can let Abraham Lincoln's wisdom motivate us:

"A child is a person who is going to carry on what you have started... He will assume control of your cities, states, and nations. He is going to move in and take over your churches, schools, universities, corporations. The fate of humanity is in his hands."

On that we can all agree.

FOOTNOTES

1   Emerson, Speech to Phi Beta Kappa Society at Cambridge, *The American Scholar*, August 31, 1837.

2   See *Teaching Character and Virtue in Schools*, (Routledge, 2017), p.1.

3   M. Garber, *Character*, (2020), p. 102.

4   Proverbs 22:6.

5   Speech to the cadets at The Citadel in South Carolina, May 1993.

6   Aristotle, *Ethics*, Book II, i

7   C. S. Lewis, *Mere Christianity*, (Touchstone: New York, 1996) Book III, Ch. 4.

8   Quoted in Warren Bennis and Burt Nanus, *Leaders*, p. 45.

9   Helen Keller, "Quotes on Character," https://www.goodreads.com/quotes/4811-character-cannot-be-developed-in-ease-and-quiet-only-through.

10 C. S. Lewis, *Mere Christianity*, Touchstone: New York, 1996, pp. 75-77.

11 The so-called "Cardinal Virtues" Prudence, Justice, Courage and Temperance, were first discussed in Plato's *Symposium*.

12 Proverbs 3:15-16

13 C. S. Lewis, *Screwtape Letters*, (Geoffrey Bles, 1942) pp. 137-8.

14 Both quotes are from Hunter, *Death of Character*, 2000.

15 Martin Luther King, "Character plus Intelligence" (in an article written by Martin Luther King while in college), https://www.goodreads.com/quotes/7847-intelligence-plus-character-that-is-the-goal-of-true-education.

16 Thomas Lickona, *Character Matters*, (New York: Touchstone, 2004) Introduction, p. xxiv.

17 Id, *Character Matters*, p. 219.

18 Watson, *A Business and Its Beliefs*, (New York: McGraw-Hill, 2003) p. 5.

19 Thomas Lickona, *Character Matters*, (New York: Touchstone, 2004) Introduction, p. xxvi.

20 Max Weber, the father of sociology as a discipline, is credited with this distinction. See courses.lumenlearning.com, "Introduction to Sociology, Power and Authority."

21 Grant Gilmore, *The Ages of American Law*, (Connecticut: The Yale University Press, 1974) pp. 110-111.

22 Aristotle, *Poetica*.

23 James Baldwin, "Quotable Quotes", https://www.google.com/search?q=james+baldwin+quoteable+quotes&oq=james+baldwin&aqs=chrome.0.69i59j46i433j0i433l2j46j0l2j69i60.4241j0j7&sourceid=chrome&ie=UTF-8

24 Irving Babbitt, *Democracy and Leadership*, (Houghton Mifflin, 1924; Liberty Fund, Inc. 1979) p. 224.

25 Burke, *Letter to a Member of the National Assembly*, p. 791

26 All these quotations may be found at: "Quotes on Liberty and Virtue", compiled by J. David Gowdy, President, The Washington, Jefferson and Madison Institute, http://www.liberty1.org/virtue.htm#:~:text=%22Liberty%20can%20no%20more%20exist,and%20move%20without%20a%20soul.%22&text=%22Public%20virtue%20cannot%20exist%20in,the%20only%20foundation%20of%20republics.%22

27 Ibid.

28 Ibid.
29 <u>Alexis de Tocqueville</u>, *Democracy in America*, 1835.
30 This conflict is discussed in Plato's *Republic*.
31 Newman, *Christian Perfection*, Sermon Notes.
32 *Choice of Hercules*, <u>http://www.dmmserver.com/agart/978/029/9780297848332.</u>
    <u>pdf</u>.
33 Michael Novak, *This Hemisphere of Liberty*, 1992.
34 There was no explicit concept of the will as a faculty of the human soul in Greek
    thought, nor in the biblical writings. The importance of the faculty of the will
    came to the fore in Augustine's thought in the 5th Century A.D.
    In Augustine's classic autobiography, *Confessions*, he wrote of the conflict in his
    soul between sexual passion and his mind's knowledge of the good:

    "Yet I did not do that one thing which I…could have done at once, as soon as I
    had the will to do so, I should have willed it wholeheartedly. For in this case the
    power to act was the same as the will. To will it was to do it. Yet I did not do it."
    Penguin Books, 1961, p. 171

    Christian thought in the Reformed tradition downplays the role of free will going
    back to Martin Luther's *The Bondage of the Will* and Jonathan Edwards' *The Free-
    dom of the Will*.

    In most philosophical thought today, the will is seen as central in moral decisions.
    Alasdair MacIntyre was perhaps the 20th Century's leading ethical philosopher in
    the Aristotelean tradition. In his monumental text, *After Virtue*, he wrote: "The
    education of the passions into pursuit [of the good] is what ethics is all about….
    Everything turns on the character of the interior act of the will…. The true arena
    of morality is that of the will and of the will alone." *After Virtue*, 2d ed. Notre
    Dame Press (1984), pp. 162, 168.

    Dallas Willard, formerly Chairman of the Department of Philosophy, University
    of Southern California, wrote: "…life must be organized by the will if it is to be
    organized at all. It can only be pulled together 'from the inside'. That is the func-
    tion of the will…, to organize our life as a whole…."
    Renovation of the Heart, (Colorado: NavPress, 2002) 35
35 Dallas Willard, *Renovation of the Heart*, (Colorado: NavPress, 2002) p. 35.
36 C. S. Lewis, *The Abolition of Man*, (Oxford University Press, 1943) Ch. 1.
37 Matthew 6:21.
38 Proverbs 4:23.
39 C. S. Lewis, *Letters of C. S. Lewis*, (New York: Harcourt, 1966, 1993).
40 1 Corinthians 13:13; 14:1.
41 André Comte-Sponville, *A Small Treatise on the Great Virtues*, (Picador: September
    1, 2002) p. 226.
42 Victor Frankl, *Man's Search for Meaning*, Trinity Pamphlet, p.3.
43 Thomas Lickona, *Character Matters*, (New York: Touchstone, 2004) p. 9.
44 This insight is attributed repeatedly to Dr. King, but researchers cast doubt.
    The following two quotations were in fact made by him: "Now there is a final
    reason I think that Jesus says 'Love your enemies.' It is this: that love has within
    it a redemptive power. And there is a power there that eventually transforms
    individuals."

"A third reason why we should love our enemies is that love is the only force capable of transforming an enemy into a friend. We never get rid of an enemy by meeting hate with hate; we get rid of an enemy by getting rid of enmity. By its very nature, love creates and builds up. Love transforms with redemptive power." In any event, it is true that whomever any teacher would transform, he or she must first love.

45 Liz Huntley, *More Than a Bird*, (Salthouse, 2015).

46 Teddy Stoddard, https://achieve.lausd.net/cms/lib/CA01000043/Centricity/domain/625/pdfs/social%20awareness/Article-Power%20of%20Encouragement.pdf.

47 Marvin Berkowitz, *You Can't Teach Through a Rat*, (Character Development Group: June 1st 2012) p. 42.

48 *Hardwired to Connect: The New Scientific Case for Authoritative Communities*, Institute for American Values (2003).

49 Id., 29-30.

50 Thomas Lickona, *Character Matters*, (New York: Touchstone, 2004) p. 149.

51 Augustine, *City of God*, 15, 22.

52 Steven Covey, *7 Habits of Highly Effective People*, (Free Press: 1989) p. 80.

53 Hal Urban, *Life's Greatest Lessons*, (Fireside: January 7, 2003; August 1992) p. 162.

54 Vince Lombardi, *Winning is a Habit*, (Collins: 1st edition (November 26, 1997)) pp. 63, 69. Here we quote two observations of the great coach collected in this small volume:

Mental toughness is spartanism with its qualities of sacrifice and self-denial, dedication, fearlessness, and love. The love I'm speaking of is not necessarily liking or the love that a man may have for his wife. The love I'm speaking of is loyalty, which is the greatest of loves. Teamwork, the love that one man has for another and that he respects the dignity of another. The love I am speaking of is charity.

The obvious difference between the group and the man who leads them is not in lack of strength, not in lack of knowledge, but rather in lack of will. The character, rather than education, is man's greatest need and man's greatest safeguard because character is higher than intellect. While it is true the difference between men is in energy, in the strong will, in the settled purpose, and in the invincible determination, the new leadership is in sacrifice, it is in self-denial, it is in love and loyalty, it is in fearlessness, it is in humility, and it is in the perfectly disciplined will. This, gentlemen, is the distinction between great and little men.

55 The Ehrmann story is told in Jeffrey Marx, *Season of Life*.

56 An incisive discussion of the relation of love to happiness is in J. Pieper's treatise on love, entitled *Love*. See Chapter VI.

57 Id, p. 241.

58 Marvin Berkowitz, *You Can't Teach Through a Rat*, (Character Development Group: June 1st 2012) p. 69.

59 M. Scott Peck, *The Road Less Traveled*, (Simon & Schuster, 1978), p. 264.

60 M. Berkowitz, *Primed for Character Education*, (Rutledge, 2021), p. 22.

61 Ibid, p. 21.

62 See Romans 5:3; James 1:2-4.

63 M. Scott Peck, Ibid p. 268.

64 Ibid, pp. 270-1.

65 J. D. Hunter, *The Death of Character*, (Basic Books, 2000), p. 227.

66 Y. Levin, *A Time to Build,* (Basic Books, 2020), pp. 194-5.

67 D. Brooks, *The Road to Character,* (Random House, 2016), p. XIV.

68 Ibid p. 262.

69 Quoted in Hunter, *The Death of Character,* 1d, p. 19.

70 See Introduction to Aristotle, *Politics,* (Oxford, 1995), p. xxiii.

71 A. Solzhenitsyn, See Brainy Quotes.

72 Theodore Roosevelt, "Brainy Quotes", https://www.brainyquote.com/quotes/theodore_roosevelt_147876